Violent Men,
Violent Couples

Violent Men, Violent Couples

The Dynamics of Domestic Violence

Anson Shupe
The University of Texas at Arlington

William A. Stacey
The University of Texas at Arlington

Lonnie R. Hazlewood
The Family Violence Diversion Network
Child and Family Service

Lexington Books
D.C. Heath and Company/Lexington, Massachusetts/Toronto

Library of Congress Cataloging-in-Publication Data

Shupe, Anson D.
  Violent men, violent couples.

  Bibliography: p.
  Includes index.
  1. Family violence—United States. 2. Conjugal
violence—United States. I. Stacey, William A.
II. Hazlewood, Lonnie R. III. Title.
HQ809.3.U5S58 1987   306.8   86–45571
ISBN 0–669–13706–5 (alk. paper)

Published simultaneously in Canada
Printed in the United States of America
International Standard Book Number: 0–669–13706–5
Library of Congress Catalog Card Number 86–45571

The paper used in this publication meets the minimum requirements of Amercian National
Standard for Information Sciences—Permanence of Paper for Printed Library Materials, ANSI
Z39.48–1984. ∞™

86 87 88 89 90 8 7 6 5 4 3 2 1

Contents

Figures and Tables

Figures

Tables

Preface

This book may be regarded as a sequel to our first book on family violence, *The Family Secret: Family Violence in America* (Boston: Beacon Press, 1983). That first book, with its focus on the victims of family violence, received a number of favorable reviews and an overall positive response from activists in the women's shelter movement. We advocated more shelters as well as additional public and private support for them.

In this volume we shift attention to the perpetrators of violence, both men and women. Our basic argument is that family violence is overdetermined—that is, it has a number of separate causes that frequently interact. While we examine a number of institutional influences, such as military service and religion, there is no way in one volume to cover the entire spectrum of contributing factors. Our purpose, therefore, is to expand understanding of this problem, not to provide definitive solutions.

We also hope to raise issues that often have been buried or not adequately confronted. Our research since *The Family Secret* has introduced and sensitized us to how politicized the family violence field has become. Studies on violent men, women, and households seemingly have posed a double threat to some women's advocates: first because money that would otherwise go to women's programs might be spent on counseling programs for persons who are not victims of violence or not women; second because male sexism is not always found to be the root or only cause of men's violence against women.

We anticipate conflict and polarization around such issues in the future, as priorities must be set in the face of limited public funds. The outlines of this struggle have become clear, as we argue in the final chapter, and its effects are already being felt. We deplore this conflict and urge everyone concerned to set aside ideological interests to consider the growing information base about the long-range dynamics of family violence. Nothing gives the detractors of any social movement more ammunition than internal bickering and factionalism. As everyone in the family violence field is well aware, a host of right-wing politicians, fundamentalist ministers, and antifeminists waits in the wings ready to exploit these disagreements.

We see the information presented in *Violent Men, Violent Couples* as contributing to a more realistic approach to solving family violence. For that reason we have presented our findings in a way that will be most useful to general readers, counselors, judges, law enforcement officers, and clergy as well as scholars and teachers. To the extent that such persons become more sensitized to the family violence problem and better informed about its various dimensions, we will have accomplished our purpose.

Acknowledgments

We relied on many sources in preparing this book and are indebted to a number of people. In particular, we wish to thank Robert Bowman, Director of the Child and Family Service in Austin, Texas; John Patrick, Carol Mantooth, and Dawn Knowles of the East Texas Crisis Center in Tyler, Texas; and Drs. Jeanne Deschner and John McNeil of the Community Service Clinic in Arlington, Texas. They generously provided us with case file and anecdotal data from their counseling programs while carefully protecting their clients' integrity and identities. Ms. Pat Crawford, formerly director of a central Texas women's shelter near Fort Hood, provided invaluable service in helping us obtain information about abuse in military families. All exemplify professionalism and a nondogmatic interest in providing violent families with effective assistance.

Funds to conduct the follow-up study of violent men discussed in chapter 6 were supplied by the Texas Department of Human Resources during the summer of 1984. We are most appreciative to the staff persons of that agency for their help. In the front lines our colleagues and assistants Dennis Brown, Richard Breen, Jim Sawyer, Lynda Blakeslee, Karen Roberts, Pam Schott, and Gaea Logan-Hines helped us as coresearchers to track down the graduates of anger-control programs and their spouses. Brown and Breen also aided in preparing some topics discussed in this volume.

At the end of acknowledgment sections, authors typically issue the caveat that no one other than themselves is responsible for the interpretations of research projects. This would be misleading in our case, for all the people named above, as well as others, in some measure contributed to our analysis. Whether or not they want to identify with the views expressed here is a choice we leave to them.

Part I
The Dynamics of Family Violence

P revious research on family violence has dealt largely with its most visible and accessible participants: the victims. Women and children in shelters have been studied by sociologists, psychologists, and social workers to the point where there is no longer much question of why women endure violence in homes rather than leave, how their self-esteem and personalities are affected, or what impact spousal violence has on children.

At the same time, the perpetrators of family violence have until recently remained a virtually unknown element of the problem. Except through the indirect testimonies of battered women, their spouses have not been accessible to researchers. Nor has the possible role of women in contributing to violence been explored.

Chapter 1 presents an overview of the family violence problem: its historical antecedents in the United States and elsewhere, its inception and development as a social concern, and its status in the public eye by the mid-1980s. We analyze family violence as a social movement and, accordingly, identify its ideologies, vested interests, and conflicts. We maintain that the very logic by which the women's shelter movement brought the problem of woman abuse into public awareness virtually ensured that treatment programs for violent men and even violent women eventually would be developed.

Chapter 2 represents a mix of sociological and psychological perspectives that explores the dynamics of male violence using the largest sample of violent men yet assembled. The roles played by various stress factors in the adult lives of these men, their previous learning, and traumatic childhood experiences that shaped their personalities are considered both separately and in combination.

Chapter 3 examines what has been a largely taboo and ignored subject: women's violence toward men. This violence takes three forms: violence by women to protect themselves against violent men, women's violence that complements their mates' equally abusive tendencies, and women's violence directed at nonviolent men. The dynamics of much women's violence is remarkably similar to that of men. Indeed, in the case of many violent couples, the emotional needs, lack of communication skills, poor anger control, and psychological insecurities of one sex mirror those of the other.

Part I deals with violence at the individual or social psychological level. The impact of larger society and culture are considered but only where specific, troubled individuals are concerned. Having sorted out the various separate but related sources of violent behavior in these chapters, we will then move in Part II to wider institutional domains to consider how they confine and structure violence.

1
Domestic Violence: The Evolving Problem

Family violence . . . can be likened to a cancer, which is part of an organism but which at the same time fatally corrupts and destroys its host.

—*The Family Secret*

Late on Wednesday afternoon, July 18, 1984, a 41-year old ex–security guard James Oliver Huberty walked into a McDonald's restaurant in a San Diego suburb carrying an automatic rifle, a shotgun, and a handgun. Huberty, shouting "Everybody down! I've killed thousands, and I'll kill thousands more!" began firing at the workers and into the throng of patrons. For more than one hour Huberty went on a berserk rampage, reloading his weapons frequently as he mowed down anyone who moved. Witnesses recall Huberty's walking up and down the aisles spraying bullets, many of them armor-piercing, into the booths. He killed two children who innocently rode up to the front door on their bicycles and another woman outside before they could enter. He shot at police cars and fire trucks as they drove into the parking lot to help the victims. Before a police SWAT team sharpshooter finally killed him, Huberty slew twenty-one people and wounded nineteen others. It was the worst one-day slaughter by a single person in U.S. history. As one San Diego police officer described the bloody scene, "It's a slaughterhouse; they were just executed."

Ironically, that same day two of the authors of this book were traveling to Austin to join the third and begin an important research project contracted with the Texas Department of Human Resources. We were to evaluate three programs that counsel violent men and violent couples. Our assignment was to follow up on the men and women who had completed these programs, to see what had become of their lives and to learn whether counseling can actually cut through the patterns of violence among mates and children.

None of the backgrounds of the men we contacted in the next several months rivaled the appalling record set by James Oliver Huberty. Indeed, most people studied were not violent outside their homes. But such violence runs along a continuum, often escalating from initially milder forms to more serious acts. Given the prevalence of weapons in our society and the inability of many persons to control anger or to deal with others' emotions, the potential for serious harm and even death rarely is remote, as police officers and the staffs of women's shelters can attest.

It turned out that Huberty had been a violent husband and father. From what police later learned, there is good reason to believe that the McDonald's massacre of July 18, 1984, was a supreme expression of personal frustration and family problems that Huberty never resolved at home. He eventually turned these feelings outward onto others through a mass killing, telling his wife as he left their apartment that afternoon: "I'm going to hunt humans!"

The San Diego tragedy is symptomatic of a larger trend that we termed a cult of violence in our previous book, *The Family Secret: Domestic Violence in America*. This cult is actually a cluster of tendencies to act and react violently that are becoming all too frequent in our society. Among such tendencies are the impersonal sources of stress and frustration built into life in our urbanized, superindustrialized society. These are the pressure points with which people are increasingly unable to cope. They extend from crowded freeways to fickle economies, to alienating bureaucracies in government, businesses, and universities, to those maddening errors and confusions that computers supposedly cannot make. In response to these strains, there is a growing number of violent actions, sometimes committed out of sheer rage and sometimes out of ignorance. They translate into freeway murders where rush-hour commuters shoot each other over fender-bender accidents; into wanton acts where unreasoning hatred (as in the McDonald's massacre) seem literally to explode; and into a situation where a frustrated husband punches his wife or an exasperated mother throws a baby down on the floor. Not all violence resulting from these trends is homicidal or suicidal, but much of it could be under the right circumstances.

Thus we believe now, as we did when we initially suggested the existence of this cult and its cancerous, corrosive effect on the American family institution, that the situation continues to become worse, not better.

Reasons for Optimism

In the short time since *The Family Secret* was published in 1983, a number of encouraging developments have nevertheless occurred in the field of domestic violence. Here are four important reasons for optimism.

Public Awareness

Public awareness of the domestic violence problem has never been higher in the country. Perhaps we are approaching a time when wife beating, child abuse, and other forms of such violence are treated seriously. Meanwhile, numerous civic and church groups in communities across the country have made women's shelters a part of their volunteer and charitable agendas. Journalists have publicized the extent of the problem and the plight of victims. Family violence regularly is taught as a unit in many college courses on marriage and the family. In Berkeley, California, the city's board of education unanimously approved a high school program on domestic violence.[1] And there is more official awareness of the violence crisis. In late 1984, for example, the New York State Social Services Commission announced a toll-free twenty-four-hour hotline for victims of domestic violence. Hotline counselors provide information, referrals, and crisis counseling to callers.[2]

Even television has discovered family violence. In the fall of 1984 NBC broadcast a made-for-TV motion picture titled *The Burning Bed*. Farrah Fawcett starred in the role of Francine Hughes, a real-life physically abused Michigan housewife who in 1977 finally ended her torment by dousing her sleeping husband's bed with gasoline and setting it afire. According to Nielsen ratings, this movie was the number one show of the season.[3] Immediately after its showing, the Associated Press reported that thousands of women, apparently motivated by seeing the movie, began calling local shelters for help with similar abuse problems. Many television stations had flashed telephone numbers for local shelters and hotlines on the screen during the movie. The publicity worked. One Oklahoma hotline received almost two hundred calls during the movie, and other shelters, including one in the Dallas–Fort Worth metroplex, found their telephone lines jammed for days afterward. Phoebe Soars, a staff worker at the Transition House Shelter in Cambridge, Massachusetts, reported, "I got a call from a woman whose husband had just beaten her because of the movie. He said she wasn't going to get any ideas from the movie, and he would get her first.[4]

In other cases as well the movie inspired violence. Police detectives in Columbus, Ohio, credited *The Burning Bed* with influencing a woman who shot her live-in boyfriend three times.[5] Coincidentally, that same week an Abilene, Texas, woman who had doused her sleeping husband with gasoline and set him afire (without having heard of Francine Hughes) was acquitted of murder on the ground of self-defense.[6] And there was one case of a Milwaukee, Wisconsin, husband who watched the NBC drama and then set his wife on fire.[7]

In short, the public response to this film was phenomenal. After years of feminists and concerned activists, social workers, social scientists, and police testifying at public hearings, the response proved, without a doubt, that the problem of family violence is widespread. In one sense the movie's success should have come as no surprise: The commercially minded moguls of Hollywood, with their hands on the public pulse, should be able to recognize a story with which millions of viewers can readily identify.

Political Awareness

Political awareness of the domestic violence crisis also has expanded considerably. Much of the credit must go to feminists, counselors who work in the trenches with family violence victims, and sympathetic researchers and other professionals. Part of the credit also must be given to politically alert officials who have finally awakened to the undeniable interests of their female voting constituencies, many of whom are, have been, or might be family violence victims. In addition, there are glaring economic realities of how much domestic violence costs the law enforcement establishment in terms of police time spent on disturbance calls, police injuries, and expensive prosecutions.

During 1984 the Texas attorney general took up the cause of family violence, suddenly endorsing legislation to curb this problem and speaking about his new-found concern to various women's groups. Such state-level activity across the nation has become commonplace in the past few years.

Perhaps more significantly, in the fall of 1983 President Ronald Reagan (who would be the incumbent in the 1984 election) commissioned U.S. Attorney General William French Smith to establish the Task Force on Family Violence, which would hold a series of public hearings across the nation, gather data, and issue policy recommendations. This represented something of a turnabout for a president who, up until that time, endorsed a traditional, hands-off policy toward the family and seemed to support the old-fashioned patriarchal model. Indeed, one of the first programs wiped out by the Reagan administration in 1981 had been the Office of Domestic Violence (established in 1979 by Reagan's predecessor, Jimmy Carter, to monitor the problem on a nationwide level and provide start-up funding for antiviolence programs). Many of Reagan's staunchest supporters, however, have little knowledge of, or sympathy for, the issue of domestic violence. Senator Jesse Helms of North Carolina, for example, has had some harsh words to say about helping abused women. He is on the record as once having said that shelters for battered women promote the "disintegration" of the family.[8]

Nevertheless in mid-September 1984 the task force issued its report, complete with sixty-three recommendations for monitoring family violence and for taking meaningful remedial steps. Little if anything in the report broke new ground, however, and after the high hopes raised in professionals working in the domestic violence field, the report seemed doomed to the archives, where other much-ballyhooed government reports have found a final resting place. The majority of the recommendations entailed costs that financially strapped local and state governments and that the federal government would be unlikely to assume anytime soon.

At the report's release, Attorney General Smith expressed vague concern about the general problem (such as "for too long our legal system has not adequately protected the victims of family violence. . . ."), but he also admitted that he had not even read the report. While Smith assured the media that "the federal response to this problem is coordinated and comprehensive" (without specifying just what that response was) and proclaimed that "the federal government can provide leadership on the issue" (without indicating how), he then asserted practically in the same breath that the federal government should not "mandate" the conduct of abusive parents and spouses.[9] This was a contradiction of the report's content, for eight (or more than 10 percent) of the task force's recommendations concerned federal executive and legislative actions that would make the federal government a decisive intervener in certain abuse matters.[10]

Still, most observers, whatever their hopes or pessimism, considered it a coup of sorts that federal recognition had been gained for what had for so long remained a locally combatted problem. The task force report was a detailed and well-planned document. Never again could anyone assume that the national scope of the problem had not been identified.

Legal Changes

Within the past two years, legal changes have been rapidly redefining the victimology of family violence. Virtually all the changes seem to be in a direction that will benefit women, the most frequent victims of spousal abuse, without jeopardizing men's rights. And all these changes are long overdue. For example, from 1983 to 1985:

> Local courts did not dismiss charges against widely known male celebrities who committed spousal violence. Television actor David Soul and Indianapolis Colt running back Curtis Dickey, for instance, had to face judges after being convicted of beating their wives.[11]

> The state of Washington became the seventh in the nation to require arrest if police are called to calm violence in the home, even if the victim does not want to press charges (following the example of Oregon, Minnesota, Delaware, Maine, North Carolina, and Utah). Based on the experience of the first ten weeks under the new law, the Seattle Police Department estimated that it would arrest about 2,800 persons during 1984 on domestic assault charges, compared to 387 persons in 1983.[12]

> The New York State Court of Appeals ruled 6–0 that men who force their wives to have sex with them can be prosecuted for rape. Such rulings are on the increase as all levels of the criminal justice system are becoming familiar with the facts on family violence. One New York State Supreme Court justice wrote us that recent publicity over sexual/child abuse

is reflective of a greater public awareness of the seriousness of our problem at the family level. Personally, I have had to deal with oral and rectal abuse by a divorced father of a three-year old son and have also had a variety of other family assault cases both physical and sexual. Recently I testified at a state hearing in this regard.[13]

The New Jersey Supreme Court ruled during the summer of 1984 that expert testimony on the behavior of women who had been subjected to repeated physical or sexual abuse from husbands or lovers was admissible to help establish claims of self-defense in murder cases. The particular case the justices heard involved a woman who had been sentenced to five years in prison for killing her abusive husband in self-defense with a pair of scissors. A news service reporter remarked that this decision "marked the first time that evidence on the syndrome (i.e., battered women's) had been held admissible by one of the country's key state appellate courts. . . . Such testimony, the court held by a vote of 6–1, is essential to rebut general misconceptions regarding battered women," such as the stereotype that they are masochistic or that they are somehow responsible for causing men's violent behavior.[14]

During the summer of 1985 a Hartford, Connecticut, jury awarded $2.3 million to a battered woman who had tried unsuccessfully time after time to obtain police protection from her husband. Although she had filed for a divorce and had taken out a court order barring the man from seeing or harassing her, he nevertheless persisted. Police, she claimed, treated the problem as a minor domestic dispute rather than a criminal assault—even when she was stabbed thirteen times and kicked repeatedly in the head by her husband while a police officer watched (the injuries left her scarred and partially paralyzed). Nothing was done until other officers arrived. In addition to the settlement, the jury declared the police department involved to have been negligent.[15]

The judicial view of family violence still needs much improvement, as many a defense attorney can attest. Despite encouraging decisions at the upper levels, many local judges still react to trials involving family violence in a knee-jerk traditionalist fashion. In 1984, for example, Stacey and Shupe once again appeared as consultants and expert witnesses for the defense in a Dallas murder trial (August, 1984 *State of Texas vs. Tina Moffet*. Dallas, TX).[16] Tina Moffet, a housewife, had accidentally stabbed her abusive husband, and he subsequently bled to death before the ambulance (which she called) arrived. Actually she had pulled a knife, as she had on past occasions, to make him back off during one of his violent drug/alcohol binges. At one point he stumbled and reached for her to steady himself, pulling her into him and fatally severing an artery in his thigh.

Carter Thompson, the defense attorney in the case, tried to enter sociological expert testimony on the sociodynamics of a battered woman's behavior as well as testimonies from a women's shelter staff member and even the defendant's minister, all to no avail. The judge, for whom there had as yet been no trickle-down effect of wisdom from higher courts elsewhere, ruled all such testimony inadmissible. Aghast, defense attorney Thompson asked, "Am I to understand, Judge, that no scientific testimony is admissible in this court?" "It is not," the judge curtly replied and thereupon declared all defense witnesses, in the prosecutor's terms, "irrelevant."

But Tina Moffet went free, convicted of the lesser charge of negligible homicide (a misdemeanor rather than a felony), and the jury gave her a probated sentence with only a fine. The jury members, plainly disgusted with the judge's abrupt dismissal of possibly informative testimony and the repeated efforts of district attorneys to quash attempts to introduce such evidence, said in later interviews that they decided that there was indeed reasonable doubt about the circumstances of the woman's fatal act.

Research

Research on domestic violence has mushroomed in books, professional and popular articles, monographs, and graduate student theses. In the process old myths and shibboleths are disintegrating. For example, only a few years ago professionals confidently spoke of the cycle of violence (where a child is exposed to parental violence and abuse, then repeats the pattern by abusing his or her own spouse and children or by accepting such violence) as if it applied equally to both sexes. Now we know that it is a valid concept to help explain male violence but not very useful in understanding most female victims.

No research study completely or absolutely decides a question. No experiment or survey can satisfy all aspects of a problem. But eventually the findings begin to accumulate, and in the sifting-out and replication process of science, the reliable facts begin to emerge. Happily, social science is beginning to gain closure on many of the basic facts about family violence.

The Politics of Family Violence

As we have stressed, understanding family violence is far from complete. Nevertheless, in recent years researchers have rapidly begun filling in important gaps. One of the reasons that more work must be done in investigating the various dimensions of the problem relates to the political nature of family violence. Politics in the sense most commonly used by writers on this subject refers to power differences between men and women in their relationships: who seeks control over whom, how force comes to be substituted for negotiation between spouses, and so forth. But we interpret the term *political* in a much different way.

As sociologists and historians of science have long pointed out, all knowledge is ultimately political; that is, knowledge produced by scientists can become politicized by official policymakers, quite apart from the purposes or intents of the scientists. In another sense, research knowledge ultimately is political because it is produced by men and women who are consciously or unconsciously influenced by their own personal value blinders, by taken-for-granted cultural assumptions, and by vested interests, egos, and career aspirations. Thus, people who produce knowledge are themselves embedded in the prejudices and cultural limits of their particular time and place, a fact that inevitably colors their lives. One has only to look back at how turn-of-the-century Anglo-Saxon psychologists and sociologists interpreted eastern and southern European immigrants' low scores on I.Q. tests as proof that these persons were genetically and mentally inferior to appreciate the pervasive effects of the everyday assumptions of one's culture and society. These social scientists were, by today's more enlightened standards, racist and ethnocentric.

Any understanding of human behavior is constructed by persons who are never completely neutral to what they study. While the general public may hold some naive faith in the sacred cow of absolute scientific truths, the longer haul perspective demonstrates that such truths often are matters of interpretation. Every current state of knowledge is relative and incomplete, based on some model of how the world works. One scholar called such models paradigms. A paradigm helps organize knowledge and influences observers in how they ask questions about the world. Yet paradigms, or models, also block out and stifle other questions that are never asked. Gaps in research begin to accumulate. Eventually these gaps become too numerous to ignore and may even contribute to the collapse of one paradigm and its replacement by another. In this way scientific knowledge constantly evolves and regenerates itself.[17]

The family violence problem likewise is a creature of the historical period in which it has been recognized. If the war against violence in the family is seen as a social movement, then like all such movements it must have an ideology. And ideologies like theologies in religion, come in many dogmas. This basic point often has been ignored by many who write on this area. They choose instead to speak of what is known about family violence as if there were simply facts with no reflection on the political context in which these facts became known. There has been an aversion to openly discussing the politics of family violence.

Because many of the topics and interpretations in the chapters that follow depart radically from past knowledge about family violence, we believe it is important to consider candidly the evolution, or emerging history, of family violence as a recognized societal problem. Only then will the directions that research in the field is now taking assume their true significance.

Family Violence in U.S. History

Awareness of family violence is not new in the United States. Just as immigrants to the original thirteen colonies on the eastern seaboard brought with them an Old World legacy in language, religion, and forms of government, so they also imported a legal tradition that recognized a husband's prerogative to discipline his wife physically if he chose. As two Scottish sociologists observed about both the United States and Great Britain, "Prior to the late 19th century it was considered a necessary aspect of a husband's marital obligation to control and chastise his wife through the use of physical force."[18]

This view can be traced back as far as the Roman Empire and medieval times in "laws of chastisement" found in many countries as well as in selected passages of the Old and New testaments in the Bible endorsing male authority over women. In *The Family Secret* we noted:

> Through the Roman Catholic church this biblically supported view made its way into European society and law. The idea of a man managing and controlling his family, disciplining both wife and children by right if in his opinion they deserved it, found fertile soil for acceptance. For many centuries, during the Dark and Middle Ages as well as the Renaissance, women were routinely subjugated. The physical punishment that accompanied their accepted inferior status, justified by the so-called "laws of chastisement," went unquestioned, though today we would consider it abuse. Such violence was simply taken for granted as part of the divinely ordained order of things.[19]

Attitudes that condoned wife beating (and similar mistreatment of children) entered into mainstream American culture via English law. The infamous rule of thumb, which permitted a husband legally to beat his wife with a rod not thicker than his thumb was a formal section of British Common Law. Ironically, it was originally intended as an example of compassionate reform to limit how harshly men abused their mates.[20] Thus men's right to use violence in managing their homes became an accepted part of colonial America and later the emerging United States. By the early 1800s many state supreme courts began to recognize this male prerogative. In 1824 Mississippi, soon followed by others, gave wife beating legal protection.

Yet the tide of legal opinion began to shift only a generation later. By the 1870s courts in New England as well as in the South started reversing their views of the appropriateness of wife beating, calling it cruelty instead of a male's privilege. Many states adopted harsh punishments for wife abusers that make today's misdemeanor fines seem tame by comparison. A Maryland law in 1882, for example, proscribed forty lashes or one year in prison for wife beaters. Delaware passed a law in the late nineteenth century decreeing that wife beating be punished with five to thirty lashes at a whipping post, while New Mexico's law against woman abuse handed abusers fines ranging from $255 to $1,000 or prison sentences of one to five years. By 1910 only eleven states in this country did not permit divorce for reasons of one spouse's cruelty toward the other.[21]

In the early twentieth century family violence as a critical social problem largely went underground once again. Despite the women's suffrage movement and the so-called liberation of women during the 1920s, family violence did not remain in the public conscience. Historians have not really figured out why. Undoubtedly, the series of world wars, economic recessions, and depressions, along with the reforms that removed many of the grosser urban horrors (such as unrestricted child labor and nonunionized sweatshops,) competed with the violence problem as major concerns. Perhaps the problem was simply too endemic and widespread at some level in too many families, including those of lawmakers, to be regarded as an outstanding worry.

In recent years awareness of family violence, especially woman abuse, has resurfaced. It is a post–Vietnam War phenomenon, a product of the 1960s that benefited from that era's inclusive concern about a broad range of environmental, racial, political, economic, and gender problems. Contemporary understanding of family violence has evolved during the past ten years through three major phases:

1. a victim-oriented phase, which until recently has been the cutting edge of antiviolence programs;

2. a direct treatment of male perpetrator phase, which recently has emerged;

3. a (family) systems-oriented phase, which is now surfacing.

The Victim-Oriented Phase

Historically, convincing anyone in a position of authority that physical violence directed by men against wives and lovers represented a major societal problem proved to be an enormous uphill struggle. As Susan Schechter describes in her excellent book, *Women and Male Violence*,[22] the women's liberation movement of the 1960s and the antirape movement of the early 1970s were precursors of the later women's shelter movement. The feminist movement sensitized many women to the inequities caused by sexism in jobs, education, mass media, and other institutions, while the antirape movement explicitly identified women as victims of male violence and established an important network through which women could speak about this victimization. Nevertheless, advocates for women who were being beaten in their own homes did not win easy recognition of this widespread problem.

Although the first shelter for physically abused women opened in 1964 through a California Al-Anon group, it was the mid-1970s before local, non-affiliated shelters began opening in cities around the United States.[23] They were established by determined feminists who launched poorly financed crusades in often indifferent or suspicious communities. There were fewer than ten shelters in the country in 1974 and only seventy-nine by 1979. By the mid-1980s there were more than a thousand.

The activists in this effort justifiably pride themselves on having brought the concept of woman battering before the public eye, for having lobbied the cause before legislators, and for having changed the attitudes of many others, including those in criminal justice and the medical professions. Since the mid-1970s millions of dollars have been allocated by legislators throughout the country to establish women's shelters, all largely as a result of feminist activists' energies. In many states and local communities, however, the task is far from complete. Many officials still regard male violence against women, particularly married women, as the subject of crude jokes or, when they encounter its raw, unsightly consequences, as some kind of grotesque aberration. Such reactions are becoming more infrequent, however, as a result of public pressure.

In sum, the victim-oriented phase identified the problem of violence in the home as distinctively one of woman battering. The lines were clearly drawn by feminists who founded shelters: Women were the victims, and men were the perpetrators of violence. Yet two important facts about how the shelter movement fits our political understanding of family violence must be emphasized.

First, this victim-focused phase (and we say nothing here about children who also are frequently the victims of violence when women are beaten) was both necessary and inevitable. Before people can be persuaded that harmful actions are being committed, they must see convincing evidence of such harm. Public ire and official motivation to act usually are aroused only by the sensational and the dramatic. Shelter advocates provided this tangible evidence, often in shocking and gruesome detail, at public hearings as well as in magazine articles and books. Women and children have proved to be sympathetic victims whose plight provokes an understandable call for something to be done for them.

Second, many persons who spearheaded the effort to establish shelters and win public recognition of the women-battering problem have explicitly claimed to be doing more than merely providing a needed social service. With the feminist movement and other minority activism of the 1960s as models, they have referred to this crusade for abused women as the shelter movement. In short, there has always been a sense of radical feminist opposition to the larger male-dominated status quo, or male oppression, running through the shelter movement. Some, like Susan Schechter, openly identify themselves as socialist feminists and proclaim that woman abuse will never end until the oppressive conditions of capitalism itself are ended. Schechter refers to the radical feminist element as helping to maintain a necessary tension, meaning that shelters should do more than simply provide havens for abused women who have nowhere else to go. Rather, they also should be crucibles in which to change, sensitize, and politicize battered women, making them aware of sexism in male-controlled social institutions. Shelters should render women unwilling not only to return to abusive spouses but also to tolerate a sexist society that implicitly condones such violence. Otherwise, as Schechter told an audience of Texas shelter workers, "when we see ourselves only as providers of service rather than as agents of social change and organizers of women, our shelters become an end in itself [sic]."[24]

The shelter movement has not always maintained this social tension, particularly as more and more shelters become managed not by radical feminist volunteers and former abuse victims but by career social workers, psychologists, and counselors. In fact, in a conservative era of severe cutbacks in much government funding for social services, the family violence field has been a genuine growth industry for many otherwise unemployed social workers. Entire careers are now being carved out of the woman-abuse problem. And tension with society is difficult to maintain when a movement must continually ask for charitable contributions and grants. Schechter deplores this cooptation of woman abuse by professionals. She claims that the same thing happened to the volunteer feminist antirape crusade when "with infuriating speed and seemingly out of nowhere traditional agencies and professionals showed up to work on rape."[25]

In an important sense Schechter is right: Professionals erode the ideological zeal for the shelter movement, for professionals are trained to respect, if not pursue, scientific inquiry. And even a paradigm-limited science resists the dogmatic blinders that ideologies try to impose. The influx of professionals into the family violence field is what ultimately pushed the understanding of how to deal with the problem into the next two phases.

The Direct Treatment of Male Perpetrators Phase

It was not long after shelters experienced a virtual avalanche of prospective clients requesting admittance, many of whom had to be placed on waiting lists for lack of room, that the ultimate futility of shelters as a sole remedy for violence against women came to be seen. To be sure, shelter advocates had always pressed for stricter enforcement of assault laws and stepped-up criminal prosecution of abusive men. (More radical spokespersons, like Susan Schechter, call for a total restructuring of the entire U.S. capitalist system.) Few shelter advocates ever thought more and bigger shelters alone would solve or even contain the problem.

To many thoughtful persons, including judges, police, and feminists, it became obvious that some direct contact had to be made with violent men if the source of the problem was to be addressed. For some abused women the shelters were simply revolving door experiences. In other cases shelter workers discovered that the same men had sent different abused women, one after another as these men changed relationships, to such overcrowded havens. Feminist activists began to call for men to take responsibility for ending men's violence against women.

Offering help to abused women remained essential, but reaching violent men was the strategy with the most long term promise for ending male violence. Starting in the late 1970s and early 1980s, a number of pioneering counseling programs, such as EMERGE in Boston, RAVEN in St. Louis, Batters' Anonymous in Redlands, California, and FOCUS in Greensboro, North Carolina, opened on a voluntary basis to male clients. In addition, many programs for men were started by women's shelters, which saw such counseling as a natural extension of a mission to help abused women and challenge sexism in the United States.

Such programs did not win immediate acceptance. Programs that rely on men's voluntarily seeking help often see ludicrously low numbers of clients. In one case a Texas women's shelter offered free counseling to violent men and received only one male client in a year's time. The numbers have been nearly as unimpressive in other instances, especially considering that women's shelters are turning away more and more women for lack of space. Many programs of this nature have closed down because of lack of response and funds. Boston's EMERGE, one of the oldest and best known voluntary programs for violent men, published a directory in 1982 containing almost two hundred agencies purportedly serving such clients. Only one year later, more of these had ceased to exist than answered a survey on men's program services sent out by researchers.[26] The underlying reason is inescapable: Most programs for violent men are voluntary, and most violent men do not believe that they have a violence problem.

Another source of resistance has come from feminists and shelter workers still preoccupied with the consciousness and problems of the victim-oriented phase. To outsiders it might seem logical for programs serving both violent men and their victims to coexist and even cooperate within the same community, but to some shelter advocates men's programs are perceived as a threat, yet another competing drain on the limited funds to help abused women. Some social workers with employment interests in the shelter movement see men's programs as siphoning away public funds and weakening their agencies. Women's advocates fear that men's programs will be managed and controlled by men—not necessarily ideologically feminist men—who set goals and use counseling techniques different from those women prefer. On this point, author Schechter says,

> Anger has erupted when programs for men received funding without enduring the severe credibility tests women's organizations have faced for years. Fury has increased as professional counseling agencies, new to the issue, tout programs for batterers even though no studies have proven the long-term effectiveness of counseling. Moreover women remain politically skeptical, concerned that counseling individual men will be viewed as a panacea and serve to discredit a feminist analysis that declares violence a result of male domination, not pathology.[27]

As a result there has developed a distinct tension and even mistrust between many (though not all) counseling programs for violent men and local women's shelters. One response by some shelter advocates has been to retain a radical feminist mindset in an attempt to protect their hard-won gains. When this has not been expressed as outright opposition to men's programs, it has meant attempts to keep them under the strict control of women's advocates. For example, feminist guidelines for funding programs for batterers, developed together by shelter activists and EMERGE counselors in Boston, were presented at a 1980 conference titled "Domestic Violence Prevention: Treatment for Batterers." Among the guidelines were statements that no men's programs should be funded in any community without the prior existence of a shelter, that shelters should always have funding priority over men's programs, and that programs for abusive men "must share the same philosophical understanding of the reasons for violence against women" as do the shelters.[28]

Another, more explicit set of feminist guidelines for assessing counseling programs for men who batter, printed by the Pennsylvania Coalition Against Domestic Violence in 1984, warned that "[C]ounseling of men who batter is becoming a popular and lucrative profession." Therefore, in the interest of helping screen out inappropriate programs, the coalition suggested a number of transparently ideological questions to ask in checking out the validity of any men's program, typical of which are the following:

> "Does the program clearly state that men's violence is chosen? . . . that violence is merely a mechanism to assert, maintain or gain control and power over women?"

> "Have all counselors had training in feminist analysis of battering and sexual assault prior to working with men who batter?"

"Does the program acknowledge the leadership of battered women and the battered women's movement in ending violence against women?"

"Does the (local) battered women's program review and approve all written materials and publications of the counseling program before distribution?"

"Do advocates from the battered women's program regularly attend group counseling sessions for men . . . [and] is there a time after each counseling session when the advocate is asked to give feedback on the group?"[29]

Other responses from shelter advocates question the autonomy of men's programs out of concern for women's safety. One piece of women's shelter folk wisdom, still commonly accepted as truth in the mid-1980s, has been that violent men frequently become even more violent during the onset of counseling, allegedly because of the pressures of reflection, guilt, confrontation, and constraint. Thus the presumed need for shelters to monitor such counseling is defended on this ground.

In sum, the direct treatment of perpetrators phase in the evolution of the understanding of family violence suggests that any effective approach to decreasing such violence must target men directly for counseling. This awareness is a major departure from the victim-oriented phase, for it has set in motion the development of a related but parallel set of social services, for the most part run by professionals rather than former abusers or volunteers and often no longer under the direct control or influence of women's shelter advocates. In other ways, however, this second phase represents an important continuity with the first: Perpetration of violence is still regarded as exclusively male (unless women act in self-defense, which is considered nonproblematic), and victimization is still considered exclusively female.

The Systems Phase

The systems perspective is just emerging, though there are counseling programs now in existence across the country that exemplify it. The strategies for dealing with violence are more complex, and therefore more controversial, than in other phases because the systems perspective does not assume that violence is basically one-sided (male). This third phase admits that women are as capable of initiating violence as men and that family units can be as violent as individual family members. Even in families where only one member is violent, this perspective recognizes a dynamic relationship that frequently exists between men and women and feeds on violence.

The logic of the systems phase rejects the feminist assumption that only the male ever needs counseling to halt violent tendencies and that it is solely his problem. The social context of the violent person is considered, and the form of therapy appropriate to the severity and extent of violence is matched with the context in which it occurs. For example, family-oriented counseling approaches might be the best treatment for the traditional family if the violent person does not have a history of violence or criminal acts outside the home. Such an approach might not be the most effective approach for a single man, however, or for men who have been violent in virtually all their relationships. Some violent individuals have what counselors term skill deficits (for instance, problems communicating with others); yet others exhibit poor impulse control in many different situations. Anger-control techniques would be more useful for the second type of problem than for the first.

The systems approach offers a more flexible definition of domestic violence, for unlike the earlier victim-oriented and direct treatment of male perpetrators phases, it does not cite sexism as the source of all forms of such violence.

Generally speaking, the shelter movement ideology, more than any other single factor, has inhibited defining domestic violence as family violence and insisted that the problem is simply one of woman battering. Spokespersons for the shelter movement originally found male-oriented attitudes regarding woman abuse so entrenched that they were forced to portray men as the only serious violent perpetrators. Those who dared suggest that women or families—not just males—could be violent were accused of sexism.

The systems viewpoint has the important negative consequence, laments feminist Susan Schechter as she anticipated its emergence, of having the women's shelter movement co-opted by professionals. She writes that the grantsmen, researchers, and other professionals who have discovered the growth industry of spouse abuse have diluted its feminist implications.[30]

Actually, the emergence of the family-oriented or systems approach is more a product of research and experience than ideology. Sociologist Suzanne Steinmetz discussed the battered husband syndrome in the late 1970s, concluding that woman abuse probably is more serious because physically larger men have a definite advantage over women when they fight. She and colleagues Murray Straus and Richard Gelles conducted the first national survey of violence in American families that found just as much violence directed by women at men as vice versa.[31] In our own examination of several thousand telephone hotline calls to one Texas shelter in the 1980s, we found a number of calls from battered men seeking help with their violent wives (and sometimes asylum for themselves). After our research received local publicity, we received direct calls from such men ourselves. We only briefly noted these cases as anomalies in our earlier book, *The Family Secret*. While we initially felt the need to support the women's shelter movement by disregarding such cases, we eventually realized that such instances were more and more common as we listened to professionals who regularly counsel violent men and their wives. There were simply too many cases of violent couples whose problem would not be resolved by teaching only him new ways to control anger or communicate with other people.

Erin Pizzey, the grand dame of the women's shelter movement world-wide, has herself recently come to grips with women's violence. Pizzey is an Englishwoman who founded the first shelter movement in 1974 and recounted her experiences and thoughts on woman battering in *Scream Quietly or the Neighbors Will Hear.* Her book quickly became the bible of the women's shelter movement on both sides of the Atlantic. She eventually came to the conclusion, however, that some women, not just men, have predispositions to violence and even derive an adrenaline rush from violent episodes that literally can become addicting. Whether one accepts this chemical dependency approach or not, there are two important points to note about Pizzey's change of perspective. First, as she relates in her later book, *Prone to Violence,* she could not ignore the fact that many women, despite having other options, willingly returned to violent men and were violent themselves. Second, she also knew the damaging consequences that revealing such a conclusion would have on the women's shelter movement. She writes:

> In those days it was too dangerous to attempt to share my discoveries in the field, because it was hard enough to gain public acceptance even for the idea that battered wives needed refuge. To discuss the notion that some women were actually prone to violence, and returned to violent relationships again and again, would only have served to alienate the public from these women who were in genuine need of help.[32]

In the chapters that follow we investigate a number of topics in family violence on the assumption that the systems approach is the most useful not only for understanding this social problem but also for remedying it. This approach's primary strength lies in its emphasis on multiple paths of causation. The politics of family violence have meant that in the past single causes were proposed and sought. These included women's masochistic problems (from early psychiatrists), male sexism (from shelter movement feminists), and inherent male aggression (from bioanthropologists). Unfortunately, the only time single causes for any widespread social behavior can be isolated is when we are working in the artificial surroundings of the laboratory experiment. Under more realistic conditions, many factors run together, making neat, clean statements about causes of behavior seem simplistic.

So it is with family violence. Seeking the causes of such violence has meant that we must abandon single-cause explanations such as sexism, psychological insecurity, media influence, and economic strains and yet simultaneously embrace them all. In a fight between a man and a woman, as later chapters will reveal, many factors are involved, some more immediate and some at work longer but each playing a role in determining how the violence unfolds.

This newest phase in the development of understanding family violence is coming of age. It is the perspective, whether named as such or not, of many male and female therapists now working in the field. It opens up the counseling situation to the possibility that women and couples, not just men, can be violent and that they are important factors in improving the violent situations.

In the next chapter we examine violent men in counseling, a focus characteristic of the direct treatment of perpetrators phase within the development of the violence problem. Having established the social psychology of that group, we will then be in a stronger position to ask similar questions about women and so move into the systems phase of investigation.

2
The Violent Man

From now on we'd better openly identify both of you as professors.
At the last session some of the guys thought you might be parole
officers.

—Hazlewood to Shupe and Stacey
before a group counseling session
for violent men

I n February 1985, John Fedders, chief enforcement officer of the Secu-
rities and Exchange Commission (SEC), resigned his post. The reason
was significant: It had become widely known through his divorce pro-
ceedings that Fedders was a longtime wife abuser. After listening to President
Ronald Reagan promise a crusade against spouse abuse in his 1984 State of
the Union address, Fedders's wife Charlotte had written a three-page typed
letter to the president detailing how she had suffered numerous bruises and
black eyes, a broken eardrum, and a wrenched neck from beatings by her
husband during their eighteen years of marriage. Once he had struck her in
the abdomen while she was pregnant with her first son and yanked her by
the hair over a banister in their house. John Fedders also psychologically
abused her, isolating her from friends and crushing her self-esteem. He closely
monitored how she spent money and her time to the point that she was
afraid to have friends call when he was home.

Already embroiled in a bribery and conspiracy trial, Fedders resigned
from the SEC under pressure both from the White House and women's
groups. Not all feminists demanded his resignation, however. As Nancy King,
deputy director for the Center for Women Policy Studies in Washington,
D.C., observed, "If we start firing all the men who beat their wives, the
unemployment rate is going to skyrocket."[1]

The Fedders incident is important because it confirms the often-heard
claim that spouse abuse is not the monopoly of poor or lower class persons.
In fact, physicians who work in the Washington area and see the victims of
family violence say that a list of abusive men would look like a *Who's Who*
of Capitol Hill luminaries. Yet as Dr. Saul Edelstein, head of emergency
services at George Washington University Hospital, testified at a public hearing, the wives of prominent men in Washington are unlikely to report any
beating by their husbands. He said:

[W]ives of congressmen will admit [being beaten] to nurses, but they don't want that on their charts. . . . Battered wives in Washington refuse to report their husbands because the publicity could ruin their spouses' careers, cutting back their own source of income. . . .[2]

The Study of Men's Violence

Whether the crime is rape or robbery, most research focuses on victims rather than on perpetrators, simply because victims are easier to locate. In recent years this has been particularly true in the family violence field as hundreds of shelters and service centers have sprung up around the country. Such shelters are places where large numbers of victims can be conveniently interviewed.[3]

Alternatively, there has been little systematic study of violent men because they are not so easy to find. Trying to interview many distraught, angry husbands of women in shelters (especially when they know that the interviewer knows where their wives are hiding) obviously is impractical. Likewise, simply drawing a random sample of all men in a community with a survey hoping to find violent men (even if they will admit it) is an inefficient approach. Our knowledge of the physical damage and emotional trauma such men cause women is enormous. But understanding what makes the violent man tick, based on studying sufficient numbers of such men, is only beginning.[4] As a result, much of what has been thought about violent males is based on speculation, ideology, or second-guessing. As one recent *Time* magazine feature story on family violence observed, "The batterer appears to have fallen through the cracks."[5]

This chapter and the remainder of this book attempt to reverse that trend. Our first step will be to examine 241 known violent men, the largest number yet examined in one study, supplementing their cases with information about 542 other violent men taken from in-depth interviews with their wives or girlfriends. Our goal is to gain a basic understanding of why these men batter women. What are their motives, their social circumstances, and their feelings about the victims and their own violence?

This emphasis on male violence is admittedly one-sided, for women and couples also can be hostile and violent. In later chapters we will take up the subject of violent women and violent households. Here we narrow our focus to the most frequent and injurious perpetrator of violence: the man.

Three Programs That Counsel Violent Men

Counseling for violent men and couples is relatively new in the family violence field. Some programs, such as Boston's EMERGE, have been in exis-

tence longer than many women's shelters, but these are exceptions. Most men's programs were recently formed and are still sorting out what works and what does not in transforming men's proclivity to violence.

For fact finders such as ourselves, these programs are invaluable. Just as women's shelters give us access to large numbers of family violence victims, so the newer counseling programs provide a unique avenue to study violent men firsthand. We found the violent men for this study in the following three Texas counseling programs.[6]

Austin Family Violence Diversion Network.

Over a period of four years we were given access to the files and the counseling sessions of the Austin [Texas] Family Violence Diversion Network (an affiliate of that city's Child and Family Service agency). The Austin diversion program was established in 1981 to handle domestic violence cases where women filed assault charges against husbands and boyfriends, the men were found guilty, and the presiding judge and district attorney agreed to defer adjudication (that is, not impose conviction for committing a class C misdemeanor—with a $200 fine and/or imprisonment—on the man). The condition was that the assaulter agreed to enter the city's four-month program for counseling. All men were first screened by a counselor. If admitted, they agreed to complete the program and pay a $50 fee. If a man successfully completed the various phases of the program, the assault charge remained on his police record, but no conviction was ever recorded and any fines or sentences were waived. If a man dropped out of the program, a warrant was issued for his immediate arrest, and he went back to court to show good reason why he should not face conviction. Over time the program came to accept volunteer admissions, or walk-ins, but the majority of men being counseled were those who had been arrested and charged with assault.

Austin's program involved men initially meeting in groups of twelve to eighteen each, with one or more counselors, and passing through three phases of counseling, each lasting six weeks. The first phase centered on teaching anger-management techniques (how to recognize buildups of frustration, anger, and rage and how to block these with methods such as meditation, biofeedback, and breathing exercises). The second phase was educational, emphasizing communication skills and basic psychological and sociological elements of sex role relationships (for example: What is it like to grow up male in American society? What kinds of ideas about men have we come to assume?). The third phase was therapy-oriented and tailored to the individual needs of clients, such as marriage counseling or alcohol and drug problems.

Altogether we examined 194 cases from Austin's program involving men who had entered and graduated between the fall of 1981 and the summer of 1984.

Tyler Family Preservation Project

The Tyler Family Preservation Project began in the spring of 1982 and along with that city's women's shelter, was part of the East Texas Crisis Center. The project's counseling emphasis was on working with families, not simply individuals, who experienced violence. Unlike the Austin program, all clients were volunteers, many of them referrals from other social service agencies.

Also unlike the Austin program, the Tyler program had no fixed termination date or separate phases. The format was simple: male and female counselors met with individual couples and established close relationships. The program emphasized confronting men and women with the reality of their fears, suspicions, and motives and leading them to communicate to their spouses honestly about needs and desires. Techniques of anger management were introduced throughout counseling sessions. Altogether we obtained information on twenty-seven violent men counseled by the Tyler program between the spring of 1982 and the summer of 1984.

Arlington Anger Control Program

The Arlington Anger Control Program was the first service to address the needs of perpetrators (as opposed to victims) of family violence in that north-central Texas region known as the Dallas–Fort Worth metroplex. Begun in the summer of 1981, the program closed the following year and then re-opened in 1983.

Like the Tyler program, Arlington's clients were restricted to couples, not individuals, who had experienced physical violence and who had come either as walk-in volunteers or as referrals from attorneys, physicians, and social service agencies. Unlike Tyler's program (but similar to Austin's), the Arlington program operated according to a definite format and sequence of sessions. The first five to seven weeks consisted of anger-control/stress-reduction lectures, demonstrations, and exercises. The second five weeks were more unstructured and focused on building skills introduced during the earlier weeks. Unlike either the Austin or Tyler programs, however, Arlington's program counseled couples in groups (though clients could have individual sessions with counselors). Altogether we obtained the case information on twenty men counseled for two years in 1981 and 1983–1984.

General Considerations

The confidentiality of every client in all three programs was respected. No name was ever entered into our computer, and every client name referred to in this book is a pseudonym. In many cases we changed irrelevant background details about the man, or family to guard further against any violation of privacy. Occasionally we combined details of two cases to obscure identities further.

There was considerable overlap in the ways the three programs were structured. All three programs were eclectic in their styles, theories, and techniques. This fact reflects the personal goals of the counselors, who were more interested in stopping domestic violence and helping clients begin more positive, enjoyable lives than in forcing those clients' problems to conform to some preformed ideology or theory. For example, all three programs helped clients forge new tools for managing anger, coping with stress, and better articulating (both telling and listening) personal needs and desires. They encouraged honest reflection on the roles men and women play in our society. They enlightened mates as to other options that could turn marriages from potentially lethal (and certainly unsatisfying) situations into meaningful, growing experiences. They quite likely even saved some lives.

In addition to these three programs, we tapped one final source of data. We already had collected files on 542 cases of battered women who had fled to shelters in the Dallas–Fort Worth metroplex after men had assaulted them. The histories of these women, and of the men with whom they lived, were collected on a standardized entry form required by the Texas Department of Human Resources.[7] While such data on violent men are admittedly secondhand, it will be useful to consider them alongside our more direct data if only to see how closely our sample of violent men (whose wives and girlfriends rarely went to women's shelters) conforms to what is known about the husbands and boyfriends of shelter residents.

The Violence the Men Committed

It is useful to have some clear overview of these men's violence before considering why they did these things. All the men we studied had been physically violent. Their actions ranged from throwing things at women and smashing objects to intimidate them, to actually striking the women. Table 2–1 lists the frequency of different kinds of violence that occurred. We did not merely take the men's word for what they did but used shelter and hospital reports, the women's accounts, and court and police evidence.

All the men had been verbally abusive (used swearing and name-calling) toward women. (It would be a frightening man indeed who could beat a woman without uttering a word of anger.) The majority of men had kicked and punched women as well as smashed and thrown things during arguments. This was true of men who had participated in counseling and those who had not. Slightly more than half the men in both groups had choked the women, and in each group the women had been battered while pregnant a third of the time. The same was true of sexual abuse (rape and forced sexual intercourse—vaginal, oral, and anal). The only important difference

Table 2–1
Types of Abuse Committed by Violent Men

Form of Abuse	Violent Men in Counseling		Violent Men Not in Counseling	
	N	%	N	%
Verbal	58	100.0	67	100.0
Kicks	29	70.1	54	80.0
Punches	32	78.1	46	69.0
Burns	6	14.6	6	9.0
Sexual abuse	13	31.7	20	30.0
Threats on life	29	72.5	35	52.0
Destruction of property	28	68.3	39	58.0
Choking	23	56.1	36	54.0
Battering while pregnant	14	36.8	25	37.0

in levels of violence seemed to be that men in counseling had threatened to kill the women in seven out of ten cases compared to the husbands or boyfriends of shelter women who had threatened them half the time.

In short, many of these men had dealt out beatings that seriously injured women, in some cases just short of killing them. It is not surprising, therefore, that many of these batterers were less than candid about admitting violence when first interviewed by counselors. Many men flatly denied that they had ever hit the women, minimized the harm they had done, or tried to justify their violence. In *The Family Secret* we found that half the time women in shelters said that their husbands or boyfriends felt that the beatings were justified (even when these same men apologized after a quarrel).[8] The men in this study tried the same tactics. Some may have felt ashamed of their actions and attempted to convince themselves that they were blameless even if no one else believed them. Others genuinely may have thought that a slap or shove was insignificant.

From the Austin diversion program we selected 119 cases that had sufficient details of the violence committed, along with the men's versions of what happened; testimony from the women, police, hospital authorities, and probation officers; and the counselor's notes. We discovered that when these men first entered the program, 70 percent had denied, minimized, or tried to justify their violent acts. That means that only slightly less than a third (30 percent) did not contest the fact that they had assaulted their wives or girlfriends. Consider these actual cases (as described by the counselors) in which men tried to avoid confronting what they had done.

Outright Denial

Dave had an injury to a child charge filed against him. He claimed he had been drinking and tried to convince his wife to go barhopping with him.

She was holding their baby, he said, when he pushed her and she fell on top of the infant, bruising its back. Her story, backed by court evidence, was that under the influence he abused her with slaps, pushing, and hair pulling before jerking the child away from her and throwing it toward the sofa (which it missed, hitting the floor).

Ted states that he is very jealous of his wife Pat, largely because he has had affairs and is afraid she will do the same. He works nights, she has friends over, and the last time he went through a buildup of worry and jealousy and beat her up. He pushed, slapped, dragged her around the floor, and punched her. He loosened her teeth, bruised her ribs, and blackened her eyes. He states that he did not hit her, though the assault [charge] was filed and he was referred here by the judge.

Sly came in on condition of probation. He is on ten years' probation for possession of drugs. Previously he was on two years' probation for burglary. He recently spent thirty days in the county jail after his wife filed a class A assault charge against him. He says he quit working at a massage parlor where his wife also works. He was at home alone, his wife had threatened to leave because of a previous fight, and he was afraid he would lose her. He got angry with himself and turned it [the anger] on her. He found her at work and pushed her down on the floor, slapped her, and stomped her head on the floor. Later, despite his own description of the violence, he states that he does not remember slapping and banging her head on the floor.

Minimization

Ted and Beth have been together for six years. He states that there have been four or five physical fights. She says there have been more like fifteen (in which he punched, slapped, shoved, and sat on her).

Bert and Karen have been married nine months and separated for the past three months. There have been three physical fights with slapping, shoving, and holding down, with each episode ending in forced sex. Basically he wants to enter the program because his wife will not return to him unless she has some evidence he will not physically or sexually abuse her. She states that he also threatened her life. He said he was only kidding.

Ed is charged with false imprisonment after kicking in his girlfriend's door and forcing her to go out with him. He states that the only thing he did was slap her on one occasion. I [counselor] talked with her, and she claims he has punched her. She has black eyes and bruises now. He tried to pressure her into dropping the charges, but she would not.

Rick and Jan have been dating for one year. (She recently spent the weekend at the Austin Center for Battered Women after Dennis told her over the phone, "If you want out of the relationship, the only way is if you die!" He states to me [counselor] that there had been five or six fights, mostly minor slapping, but she went to a doctor after one particular battering. She has had four or five black eyes, has been slapped, has had her hair pulled, and has been kicked and choked almost unconscious repeatedly.

Obviously he minimizes a lot. She filed charges against him when the last battering occurred, and he is trying to get her to drop them. He uses the excuse that he wants a job on the APD [a local community's police] force, and an assault charge will be hard on his getting the job.

Justification and Projection of Blame

Vince and Ruth have been married 6 months with continuous violence. It has been pretty severe, with Ruth having visited a doctor twice for torn lips (no stitches). Vince has threatened her life on several occasions, and she is afraid for her safety. He does typical justifying, rationalizing, and blaming her for having a "smart mouth" and not leaving him alone.

Bud blames their marital problems on her "changes" after their marriage. Previously, he claimed, she had been a religious woman, but she began drinking, dancing, and wanting sex five or six times a day. He admitted he already had the problem of impotency but said she complicated them. Thus he said he was driven to push and shove her, grab her by the hair, etc.

Juan slapped his wife when she would not do what he wanted her to do. Basically he believes that his wife caused the violence by not treating him right: "If a woman treats you right, anger doesn't come in between." He seriously minimizes violence because he states that the worst thing he has done is choke his wife and throw her down. The [Austin] Center for Battered Women intake examination shows he slapped, kicked, and choked her; pulled her hair; and punched her, resulting in multiple bruises. He also sexually abused her in front of their kids and beat one son until unconscious.

Peter slapped and punched Camille in the chest and face to make her stop "cussing" him and saying "bad things." He had asked her to stop, he said, because it was Sunday and "you shouldn't say those things on Sunday."

Many of the reasons the men gave to account for their violence are patent rationalizations. The implications are obvious, not just for counselors who must begin a major reorientation of the men's attitudes as well as their behavior but also for those wanting to gain insight into the mindset of violent men. Many persons have observed how battered women often blame themselves for the violence or deny to themselves and others that things are other than normal. Indeed, one task that women's shelter workers routinely engage in is to reshape women's perspectives and get them to stop accepting blame for being victims. Apparently there is a complementary attitude problem on the part of many violent men: They are reluctant to confront their hostility and take responsibility for violence against women.

When Are Men Violent?

The immediate issue, or precipitator, that promotes a violent argument in a home may seem incredibly trivial to an outside observer: overcooked vegetables or the same recipe served twice in one week, the announcement that an in-law is coming to visit, or an offhand comment muttered under the breath. Some men appear to be almost like animal traps with hairspring release mechanisms, needing little excuse to become destructively angry. Many battered women likewise have reported sensing that when the man was in the mood for violence, almost anything could trigger anger.

Sociology, which is the study of groups and the social (as opposed to natural) contexts in which people live, probably can never point to the final causes of family violence. Why one man batters his wife and another who resembles him closely does not can only be answered by examining their individual histories. Such answers lay more in the field of psychology than sociology. Nevertheless, there are important sociological characteristics of these violent men that point to contributing factors. Their anger was not random. They did not lash out for absolutely no reason at all, however irrational their violence might seem at first glance. By looking at some of the immediate features of these men, we can gain a sense of the stresses and strains that set the stage for violent outbursts.

The oldest truism in the family violence field says that no one segment of American society exclusively accounts for wife battering. Rich and poor, well educated and relatively ignorant, doctors and ditch diggers—all types of men can be abusive. Our findings confirm that family violence indeed runs the gamut of the U.S. economic ladder and its social pyramid. At the same time it is important to remember that the people who usually end up as clients in agencies are not truly representative of all people with a particular problems. For example, men who have more resources—money, political connections, better educations—often find ways to escape prosecution or conviction for assaulting women (besides entering counseling programs). For this reason, we see both a broad range of types of men in the three counseling programs yet at the same time more of some types than others.

Five sociological factors about these men (age, education, occupation, income, and ethnic-racial background) illustrate how certain strains helped make violence more likely.

Age

Most men in counseling were young, though the men's total ages ranged from 18 to 73 (see table 2–2). The average age was 29 years (compared to 33 years for violent husbands and boyfriends of shelter women). It might be tempting to conclude that family violence is a particular problem of the post–World War II baby boom generation, or at least more so than of older men. A better explanation for why these batterers are so youthful is that older women are not prone to file assault charges or leave violent homes for shelters either because of traditional attitudes or because of the possibility of divorce. Likewise, counselors can attest that older males are more difficult

Table 2–2
Frequency Distribution of Batterers by Age

	Violent Men in Counseling		Violent Men Not in Counseling	
Age	N	%	N	%
18–24	45	21.3	66	13.1
25–29	56	26.6	145	28.8
30–34	42	19.9	136	27.0
35–39	32	15.2	66	13.1
40–44	18	8.5	42	8.4
45–49	8	3.8	28	5.6
50 and over	10	4.7	20	4.0
Totals	211	100.0	503	100.0

Table 2–3
Frequency Distribution of Batterers by Education

	Violent Men in Counseling		Violent Men Not in Counseling	
Education	N	%	N	%
Less than high school	38	23.0	213	43.8
High school/GED	60	36.4	183	37.7
Some college	44	26.7	68	14.0
Undergraduate degree	15	9.1	13	2.7
Graduate work	8	4.8	9	1.8
Totals	165	100.0	486	100.0

to counsel and more obstinate and resistant to changing their attitudes about women. Thus there is no good reason to think that spouse abuse is unique to young men who grew up in the 1960s and 1970s.

Nevertheless, youth is a critical factor because it is a prime time of stress in men. Job security is the most precarious, and many men are gaining the first precious footholds in their careers. Furthermore, adjusting to mate and children puts enormous demands on young adults under the best conditions.

Education

Not surprisingly, we found that batterers in counseling tended to be better educated than either the mates of battered women in shelters or the average American male (see table 2–3). Almost eight out of ten men in counseling had a high school education or beyond compared to six out of ten uncounseled violent men. Comparable national figures show only slightly more than half of all American men having at least a high school education. We would expect men with more education to be more open to seeking professional help with violence or any other problem. We would expect them to recognize a violence problem in themselves, and the need to remedy it, much more readily regardless of their unwillingness to admit it openly. As we noted elsewhere in analyzing the predicament of violent men: "A low education level does not cause violence, of course, but it aggravates the frustration felt by both . . . men and women . . . when they quarrelled. Among other things, education can provide people with alternatives for resolving family disagreements.[9]

Our findings bear this out. We compared men who were pressured by judges to enter the Austin diversion program with men who voluntarily walked in to the program. The court-pressured men were less likely to have high school educations than the voluntary walk-ins. Among the men in counseling, four out of ten had some college or a college degree compared to fewer than two out of ten of the noncounseled violent men.

The point, therefore, is not that better educated men (whether we define that as having a high school or college diploma) are less likely to beat their wives but that they are more likely to recognize that they have a problem and need help.

Occupation and Income

Every job has some stress built into it, but unemployment magnifies that stress many times over. We found the unemployment rate of violent men, whether they were being counseled or not, was almost double that at the national level around the same time and more than double the Texas unemployment rate. In terms of strains that aggravate family tensions, unemployment is unquestionably a major factor.

The occupations of violent men in and never in counseling closely resemble each other (see table 2–4). Although the counseled men included slightly more clerks, skilled laborers, and salesmen, those men who had

Table 2–4
Frequency Distribution of Batterers by Occupation

Occupation	Violent Men in Counseling		Violent Men Not in Counseling	
	N	%	N	%
Unemployed/homemaker	28	14.5	74	14.9
Unskilled laborer	31	16.1	119	23.9
Clerical/skilled laborer/ salesperson	113	58.5	258	51.9
Professional/farmer	21	10.9	46	9.3
Totals	193	100.0	497	100.0

Table 2–5
Frequency Distribution of Batterers by Income

	Violent Men in Counseling		Violent Men Not in Counseling	
Income	N	%	N	%
Less than $10,000	57	33.3	139	41.9
$10,000–$20,000	73	42.7	124	37.3
More than $20,000	41	24.0	69	20.8
Totals	171	100.0	332	100.0

Table 2–6
Frequency Distribution of Batterers by Ethnicity

	Violent Men in Counseling		Violent Men Not in Counseling	
Ethnicity	N	%	N	%
White	126	59.2	309	61.0
Black	41	19.2	136	26.8
Hispanic	46	21.6	62	12.2
Totals	213	100.0	507	100.0

Note: There was an Other category, but no responses were made there.

voluntarily entered counseling (instead of being pressured by the court) had the higher prestige jobs (these included computer programmers, independent businessmen, and lawyers). Again, not surprisingly, the men in counseling tended to have higher incomes than violent men not in counseling (see table 2–5).

More so than age and education, employment (and the related income factor) reveals the importance of the situational stress factor. "The role of economic strain in aggravating family violence, making it either more severe or more frequent or both, particularly in young families where the man is struggling to establish a comfortable home for himself and his family, is undeniable."[10]

Race-Ethnicity

Finally, we classified batterers as white, black, and Hispanic (the latter a major ethnic presence in our Sunbelt region). (See table 2–6.) Contrary to popular stereotypes that wife beating is largely a minority problem, we found that both the violent men in counseling and uncounseled men related to women's shelter residents were more likely to be white (in six out of ten cases). In fact, all of the known violent men in our study had racial-ethnic backgrounds proportionate to the racial-ethnic composition of the general population. Race and ethnic origins are still sensitive topics for many Americans, and little is known about any differences in instances of family violence along racial-ethnic lines. We can at least say that such violence cuts across both majority and minority groups.

Conclusions

In sum, the five dimensions of age, education, occupation, income, and race-ethnicity have told us a few important things. They point to some of the stressful situations in which violent men find themselves. Many of the men we studied tended to be young, at points in their lives when their families and careers were still being formed. For many men this time is one of both challenge and accomplishment but also a time of frustrations, anxieties, and expanding responsibilities. Yet many nonviolent men also are caught in such stressful situations. Therefore these conditions are not sufficient to explain why some men batter and others do not. They do, however, give us some indication of when men's violence is most likely to appear and therefore when many women are in positions of greater risk.

Why Do Men Batter?

As we have seen, stress, rather than causing violence, simply makes the occurrence of violence more likely. The real roots of male violence, therefore, must be traced to experiences in the lives of the men themselves. This complicates things for two reasons. First, any generalization about a group of men will not necessarily fit every man. Every trend, even a strong trend, will have exceptions. Second, we view male violence as being overdetermined. That means that any individual man's violence is likely to be a product of more than one cause of influence working simultaneously. Practically speaking, we could expect to find that a sexist culture, a media-reinforced cult of violence, and stress could interact with the life experiences of different men in different ways.

Nevertheless, certain persistent patterns emerged from our in-depth interviews, psychiatric profiles, and discussions with the 241 men in the three counseling programs. We have separated these into four critical causes or foundations of adult men's violence:

1. physiological factors
2. trauma from abuse as a child
3. early childhood learning
4. lack of communication skills and impulse control.

As might be expected, some men showed the greater effects of one or two influences, but the majority of men reliably could have their violent behavior traced to most if not all of these sources.

Physiological Factors

The importance we should give physiological factors in accounting for men's violence is not completely clear mainly because so few persons interested in the family violence problem also have the necessary expertise in biology. As psychologist Jeanne Deschner, author of *The Hitting Habit,* reminds us, however, "the primitive rage reactions leading to aggression and battering are unlearned, instinctual patterns. Angry and aggressive responses are 'wired' into every mammalian brain as a vital part of each individual's survival equivalent."[11]

Dr. Deschner, in fact, has reviewed hormonal and dietary influences in stimulating human aggression and has employed this knowledge in the Texas anger-control program that she directs. She has found dramatic behavior changes in a few men with hypoglycemia by suggesting a change in diet (away from sugar and starches). The link seems to be between blood sugar proportions and neurochemical imbalances that result in mental depression, among other problems.

Occasionally, however, batterers have tried to pin the blame for wife battering on chemistry in an effort to shift responsibility for their violence away from themselves. The following is one example of this type of situation.

> Dave and Jane came to a counseling program after Jane had filed assault charges against Dave. In the most recent incident he had broken her nose and blackened both eyes, pushing her around while she was pregnant. He had kicked her on the buttocks and choked her, leaving visible bruises on her neck. Dave wanted Jane to have an abortion, but the doctor advised against it. Dave knew he had hypoglycemia and told the counselor that this condition made him more violent. It was really a transparent attempt by Dave to rationalize his violence, and he had repeated it often enough to his wife that she believed it and forgave him. He was not inherently violent, he argued, nor was he responsible for his violence. Rather, his blood sugar condition was the real culprit.

The connection between physiological factors and violence can be better seen when alcohol, a depressant and disinhibitor, is involved. Battered women frequently report that their husbands and boyfriends drink or that the violence escalates when the men are drunk. Again, alcohol per se does not cause violence; the majority of American men drink yet do not physically abuse their wives. In the Austin diversion program, which had the largest number of men, only a small proportion were violent solely when they had been drinking (and then fairly heavily). Most men were violent whether or not they had been drinking or not though the violent episodes after drinking typically were more severe and more frequent.

The majority of American men and women use alcohol. Given this fact, and given the disinhibiting nature of the drug, which encourages people to release emotions that they usually hold in check (whether these be amorous urges or hostility), it would be surprising if alcohol were not frequently associated with family violence. This is one reason that alcohol counseling often is paired with anger-control counseling in the three programs. It also illustrates the overlapping influence of many factors on the family violence problem.

Actual physiological disorders, such as hypoglycemia or brain tumors (which one physician suggested to us), are only a possibly important factor for a relatively small number of men in any counseling program. Future research may eventually reveal as yet unknown subtle physiological influences. But at this time it appears that most violent men are in average physical health. Certainly such factors played a minor role in influencing any of the family violence we encountered.

Trauma from Abuse as a Child

Generational transfer is the general proposition that the problems and limitations of one generation are frequently passed on to its descendents, who then experience these same problems. For example, dull parents tend to produce mentally dull children, who eventually grow up to become dull parents themselves, and so on. In the case of family violence, two aspects of generational transfer must be considered. The first is the idea that abusive parents produce psychological traumas, or emotional scars, in their children, which stay with them when they grow up and become parents.

This generational transfer of a proclivity for violence was frequently the case in the backgrounds of the men we encountered. The love/hurt/rage reactions that helpless young boys felt toward their abusive, powerful parents (for whom the boys nevertheless felt affection) were replayed by these men in their own marriages. In other words, their own experiences of callous or even cruel treatment as children could be seen as an unfortunate legacy they carried with them into adulthood, often on a level below their own awareness.

Because many of these men found their fathers to be cold, unresponsive, or indifferent, they turned to their mothers for warmth and the protective side of parental strength. Only the mothers would give the boys positive feelings of self-worth and genuine comfort. This scenario emerged from talking with the men about their home lives as children, and it was being repeated in their own homes as adults. These men typically had very little to do with their own children, particularly infants and young children, as if they were aloof from or uninterested in their offspring. Actually they lacked the ability to relate fully and effectively, just as their own fathers had.

A 47-year-old man named Don, married to his second wife at the time of his counseling, had spent fifteen of the past twenty years in prison. He was a textbook example of a man exposed to early childhood violence. He had been raised in a very violent home where his stepfather beat his mother and abused him physically as well. He recalled a number of times when his stepfather came home drunk and began pummeling his mother. When young Don tried to intervene, the stepfather turned on him as well. In the last violence involving his own wife, Don had been drinking when they began to argue about her two teenage children from a previous marriage. Don pushed her across the room, slapped her several times, and threw her against the kitchen table, cracking two ribs. Ironically, Don did not want his wife to leave and repeatedly professed his love for her. His entering counseling was part of a deal to which he agreed for her to stay.

In reality Don was emotionally dependent on his wife. This dependence probably is the most common and important residue left over from childhood abuse. It is the effect of the abusive father shutting off any meaningful affectionate relationship with his son, leaving that son no other alternative than the mother for emotional gratification. That boy eventually comes to develop a general emotional dependence on women. The violence of a man like Don, therefore, is really his crude attempt to retrieve the same feelings of warmth and security that he originally received from his mother but that his wife may not even be aware he needs. The added possibility that the mother also might have had an abusive streak herself obviously would only complicate such a man's emotions.

At first glance the emotional dependence argument may seem contradictory, given how brutally some of these men mistreat and try to dominate their wives and girlfriends. In reality, however, much of their violence is generated by their unspoken, often unconscious dependence on women for emotional strength. This was seen in man after man: The more violence in the relationship, the more dependence was present. There were several related consequences. The men, reinforced by macho themes in American culture, developed an exaggerated, rigid model of what it means to be a male. They suppressed emotional feelings that they interpreted as weak or feminine. They had little experience in communicating emotional needs and frustrations, letting these build and feed on brooding until they came out explosively as resentful hostility.

Some men felt remorseful and guilty about their inability to deal with violence and the frustrations that produced it. Although they could not easily put their feelings into words, they often hated themselves for how they had hurt their spouses. More than one man commented bitterly that he turned out "just like my dad." As one man described his feelings, "I used to be so afraid when my father started beating my mom and so helpless because I couldn't do anything to stop him. I hated him so much then, and told myself that I would never be like him. Now look at me. I am just like him."

Thus, periodically, under stress of frustration, these men unleashed violence on women close to them in a way they never could do as children against their parents. The intimacy of marriage and sexuality caused ambivalence for them. Like all persons, they sought affection and security but were already predisposed to fear being hurt. Originally in their lives being hurt meant physically as well as emotionally, followed by feelings of helpless rage.

In this light abusive men's frequent domineering behavior over women makes sense. As experts have pointed out, many violent men closely monitor a woman's time (as when she is shopping, running errands, or at work), make them account for all money spent down to the penny, forbid them separate sets of car keys or bank accounts, and even develop imaginary paramours with whom they accuse women of having affairs. Yet excessive control of the very women upon whom they are dependent is simply an attempt by these men to shore up their need for security. In one case a man installed a dead bolt lock on the outside of his house's doors. Each day when he left for work, he removed all the telephones and locked his wife in so that she would not "flirt with neighborhood men."

Such dependence paradoxically also can produce some of the worst (and most desperate) violence. Some of the men blamed their wives for real and imagined interest shown by other men. Many times they pressured their wives to be pretty and attractive but then became angry and jealous when the women dressed up. These men became violent when their dependence was threatened and sometimes when a situation might expose their vulnerability, such as when the women announced they might leave. One man in counseling had beaten his wife after she returned from a battered women's shelter, telling her, "I'll teach you what a battered woman really is!" It was the worst beating he had ever given her. Another man terrorized his girlfriend for six hours one night when she tried to leave after a violent argument. He locked the door and hit her in the head every time she tried to go to sleep. During the night he broke most of the furniture and, beside himself with fear and anger, knocked holes in the walls with his fists. This was the same man who would threaten or become violent toward whomever she went to for sanctuary. In the extreme such a man might end up killing his wife or himself. He is so dependent on her that he would kill her rather than let her go and not be able to live without her.

These dependent boys-grown-to-be-men never develop close, emotionally supportive relationships with other men. The emotionally stunting effects of their upbringing affect them even here. They tend to have few friendships. Most often it is the women in their lives with whom they share whatever amount of emotional intimacy they have, rather than with male friends. Men said things to counselors such as "She is the only one whom I can really talk to" and "Talk to my wife, she is the only one who really knows me." That is why it is so devastating to these men to have their wives leave, as shelter workers who screen the telephone calls of anguished batterers can testify. Indeed, this emotional dependence is the primary reason most volunteers entered counseling in any of the three programs. Their wives had left or threatened to leave, making the men's counseling a condition for returning or remaining.

Usually another result of their dependence was that these men had difficulty accepting personal responsibility for their actions, feelings, and thoughts. Thus they exhibited constant defensiveness in the beginning of counseling: They rationalized, minimized, and pointed blame away from themselves. In violent instances, "she" was always at fault. "She made me angry" is the most common excuse for violence heard when men first enter counseling, and in the programs we studied, it is the first element of the violent man's worldview and vocabulary that counselors assail. Violence and anger, the men repeatedly are told, are choices. There is nothing inevitable about them in the face of frustration or even provocation. They can be unlearned.

Early Childhood Learning

The second aspect of the generational transfer theory is the boy's modeling or imitation of his parents' (particularly his father's) violent behavior. Aside from any direct abuse they experienced, most of these men had witnessed violence between their parents during arguments. They saw violence used as a strategy by the father to win those arguments with the mother, or at least to get his way. They saw it portrayed as manly, as the man's right, and associated it with a male parent figure whom they naturally wanted to imitate. Thus as boys many of these men learned (indirectly or vicariously) the appropriateness of men's using violence against women as well as its effectiveness. Little in what they were to learn from American culture, either in how power and resources are distributed by gender or through the mass media with its macho heroes and docile female stereotypes, contradicted these impressions.

Not all men who had learning experiences about male violence had been abused as children. Not all had emotional problems as adults.

> Roberto, a young father in his late twenties, had taken in his younger brother's 17-year-old widow and her two small children as part of his family responsibility. The 17-year-old sister-in-law was not a responsible mother, however, and after finding that her children would be taken care of one way or another by her in-laws, she began staying in bars until early morning night after night. Roberto tried to lecture his sister-in-law on her duties to her children as well as on the courtesies she owed her hosts. She rudely

rejected his advice, so he put her over his knees and spanked her. She filed assault charges, and he was arrested.

While one could fault Roberto for his lack of tact in dealing with his sister-in-law, he certainly did not fit the profile of the typical batterer we have been discussing. Yet he was a product of the school that prescribed definite roles and duties for men and women. Raised within a traditional, patriarchal Hispanic subculture, Roberto had internalized the role of head of household in which the family's main provider by right disciplines other family members when they disobey him.

More representative was the case of Bob, a 55-year-old Austin man, married, with two grown children.

His oldest son was out of the house and doing well on his own. Bob's youngest son, 22, lived at home and worked in his father's business. Bob was the type of man whose violence mainly resided in his reactions to stress and his beliefs about a male's right to have the final authority in the family. He ran an extremely stressful service-oriented business and put in long hours. His physical violence had occurred in long cycles, about every two and a half to three years during his thirty-year marriage. Although his physical violence had been sporadic, he had used fear, intimidation, and threats to maintain control over his family. Bob's violence did not arise from anger. Rather, he became violent when he was under stress and he saw a need to restore order to his family. He described very clearly to a counselor how he used violence as a management tool in his family: "Once you've hit [your wife] you shouldn't have to do it again until she forgets." Bob unabashedly believed in instrumental violence that kept the family on edge and his wife afraid of him, thus rendering them all more compliant with his wishes.

Lack of Communication Skills and Impulse Control

Along with these men's frequent exposure to violence as a technique for getting what they want and the strong emotions generated within intimate relations because of earlier experiences, there was a third related problem. Control of anger, or use of negotiations rather than sheer physical force, rarely had been portrayed to them as virtues. Many of their fathers were not impressive models for learning how to control anger or other strong emotional impulses. Given that many of the men came into counseling not even understanding their true feelings about the women with whom they were living, it is not surprising that they were poor communicators of their feelings. The frustration of having powerful emotions that they often were unable to articulate meant that violence became a means of expression that had the unfortunate effect of depressing or driving off the very affection they sought.

In the final analysis, much of these men's violence was grounded in two character traits: emotional dependence and feelings of personal insecurity, along with low impulse control. The first trait is a product of personality formation. The second trait can be thought of as a skills problem: These men could not communicate their needs and frustration effectively. They had short fuses when it came to trying alternative ways of dealing with problems. Both traits were reinforced by a sexist culture and early life learning that proved to these men that violence is a workable, accepted style of winning disputes in intimate relations.

Other information supports these conclusions. For example, table 2–7 presents the numbers and percentages of violent men in the Austin diversion program who agreed with statements about things that might have been bothering them before they entered counseling.[12] Significant numbers of the men reported feelings best characterized as showing low self-esteem, a sense of dependence on others but also a lack of trust toward them, and a sense that they had little control over events in their lives. For example, one in four men felt that others were mostly to blame for their personal problems, were bothered by easily hurt feelings, and felt that they were trapped or caught at this time in their lives. One in four men felt that others did not understand them. More than two-thirds admitted feeling that people would take advantage of them given the chance.

Almost as many had an unhappy sense of guilt over their violence that continued to bother them even as they projected their feelings onto their mates. Sometimes this guilt took extreme directions that might seem bizarre or preposterous to outside observers. Perhaps the most imaginative case in the genre of guilt responses was Ken, a 19-year-old man who had been married a little over a year.

> Ken and his wife had an infant son. Most of Ken's violence has centered around a rather obsessional and evidently delusional sexual fantasy. He

Table 2–7
Psychological Self-Inventory

Were You Bothered By:	Yes	%
Feeling others are to blame for most of your problems	46	25.6
Feeling easily annoyed or irritated	90	50.3
Feeling trapped or caught	47	26.0
Temper outbursts you could not control	132	70.6
Feelings being easily hurt	66	36.9
Feeling others do not understand you	47	26.3
Feeling tense or keyed up	87	47.0
Having urges to break or smash things	90	48.9
Getting into frequent arguments	135	72.6
Shouting or throwing things	106	57.9
Feeling people will take advantage of you if you let them	131	70.8
Feelings of guilt	125	67.9
Feeling you should be punished for your sins	89	48.1

believed that his wife had masturbated with her son's foot while they were all in the same bed. His wife denied this. He had beaten her several times until she admitted she had done something wrong. He also accused her of trying to stimulate herself sexually while she was holding the infant on her chest and the child's feet were close to her crotch. He had also beaten his wife several times a night. His story was that he would wake up in the middle of the night and notice that the covers were moving. He knew that his wife was masturbating and he would hit her until she stopped. Her story was that she would wake up in the middle of the night with her husband hitting her. She usually would receive several knots on her head from these sessions. She also reported that when she would get up in the middle of the night to use the bathroom, he would follow her into the bathroom and accuse her of masturbating. He would also accuse her of having sexual thoughts about the baby. Ken was unable to discuss why masturbation was so bad as to demand violence, much less the notion that his wife was not masturbating and if she really were, then how did that make him feel? Eventually he was able to express his feelings that he felt very inadequate with the thought that she was masturbating. He clearly projected onto her his feelings of impotency and inadequacy, creating an almost psychotic world of sin and guilt.

Many of these men also recognized their own lack of ability to control impulsive irritability and anger. Half admitted that they were easily annoyed or irritated, felt tense or keyed up, or had urges to break and smash things. Seven out of ten men said they had temper outbursts that they could not control or got into frequent arguments.

The women interviewed at one point during the Austin diversion program's operation reported on men's behavior in various situations. Their responses, as seen in table 2–8, indicate from a woman's perspective how

Table 2–8
Batterers' Social Behavior According to Women

During the Last Month He Has:	*Yes*	*%*
Made me feel wanted and needed	44	77.2
Become upset over small things	44	78.6
Shown affection toward me	47	82.5
Displayed radical mood changes	45	78.9
Shown interest in what I say	37	64.9
Been overly suspicious of me	46	80.7
Lost his temper	57	98.3
Been more concerned about others than about me	50	89.3
Spent free time with our family members	22	39.3
Been able to accept my telling him when I am angry with him	5	8.8
Attempted to control what I think and do	48	85.7
Made it clear what he expects of me	10	17.9
Belonged to and participated in civic activities	8	16.7
Complained about his job or people he works with	36	92.3

the dynamics producing a violent male occur. The majority of the women consistently described the men as poor communicators. The men did not make clear what they expected of their wives. They tended not to show interest in the women's viewpoints, and they were generally unable to accept it when the women told them that they (the women) were angry.

The men's dependence also is evident. Eight out of ten women said that their men had been overly suspicious of them, and slightly more claimed that their husbands had made attempts to control what they thought or did. Yet more than three-fourths of these battered women reported that the men had made them feel wanted and needed and had shown them affection. This fact is not so paradoxical, given the men's ambivalent but powerful emotional dependence.

The women also agreed about the men's poor impulse control. The majority of women said that the men became upset over small things and had radical mood changes (a sort of Jekyll and Hyde effect associated with a low tolerance for frustration) when they lost their tempers. The importance of these women to the violent men grew in other ways as the men became social isolates. For instance, more than eight out of ten men did not belong to or participate in any civic organizations or activities. For them the woman, and the family, became the exclusive targets of frustration and also the sources of gratification. Finally, these men complained a good deal about their jobs and the people with whom they worked. True, griping about one's job is fairly frequent in our society, but a complaint or irritation common to a large number of men becomes a major stress factor for a man with few skills or attitudes to handle it.

Typical Behavior Patterns

Thus we see a convergence in both male perpetrators' and female victims' reports about male violence against women. Certain patterns in the men's behavior seemed to emerge, enough so that we can offer the following three descriptions of typical violent men. The first is an overall profile. The second describes men who had emotional dependence as the primary factor in their violence. The third describes those men with low impulse control and high levels of anger as the primary factor in their violence.

The Overall Profile

This man is not violent in any other areas of his life outside his home. A typical scenario involves a man in his late twenties, married for several years or living with a woman. Arguments and conflicts usually are nonsubstantive (that is, over minor issues or over implied and unspoken issues). The arguments escalate in rapid fashion to physical violence. Besides these explosions of anger and violence, the man is described by his wife as a good husband and father. He is usually a dependable and stable employee.

This man witnessed his father beat up his mother over a relatively long period of time and identified with his mother's abuse. Most such boys attempt to intervene in the violence at least once to protect their mothers. One man reported that "everytime I tried to stop my dad, he would push me out of the way or hit me. When I was big enough, I finally stopped him by beating the shit out of him when he tried to hurt my mom." Another man told a counselor that "When my dad went out drinking, I used to lay in front of my mother's door. Sometimes he would kick me to make me get out of the way."

Profile of Men with Emotional Dependence as the Primary Factor

He can be well off, around thirty. He attempts to isolate his wife from her support groups, making her financially dependent on him by either sabotaging her attempts to work or by refusal to let her work. He is very jealous and often accuses her of infidelity, using such a possibility as a rationale to beat her. He is extremely apologetic after a violent episode and often suffers guilt feelings as well as the fear that he eventually may drive her away.

Profile of Men with Low Impulse Control as the Primary Factor

This man typically is younger but not necessarily so. His violence is unpredictable from his wife's standpoint. It also is frequent and often more severe. One man's wife was blinded by a blow to the side of her head, which crushed the bone around one eye and destroyed the internal structures of the eye. He denied he had "meant to hurt her" and claimed that "I don't know what happened. I just lost control. I did it before I knew what happened."

This man has a history of losing his temper from childhood (usually modeled after the father figure in his childhood family). He has a history of fights or scraps. Often his low impulse control is combined with an equally low tolerance for frustration so that even minor conflicts escalate to major violence.

The Violent Man in Retrospect

The violent men in the three counseling programs we examined were not dramatically different from the men who batter women and drive them to seek safety in women's shelters. This fact gives us a better sense of the background to the violence occurring in many homes that occupies so much of the time of police on domestic disturbance calls, of judges in divorce courts, and (increasingly, we expect) of judges in criminal courts. We also have a better perspective now of the battering male and of his predicament.

The tragedy for many violent men is that they are caught in a vicious circle of emotional dependence that fuels their anger and ends up being counterproductive to their own needs. Like the old adage that says the tighter one grips a handful of sand the faster it runs between the fingers, so these men actually jeopardize their marriages and intimate relationships by domineering and violent attempts to hang on to their women at all costs. In many ways they are inept at expressing how they feel, which only builds their frustration. The outcome, as we have said, is paradoxical: The violent actions of bigger, stronger men bely their emotional need for smaller, weaker women's affection. They hurt what they love and often seem unable to break out of the cycle by their own efforts.

For other men the problem is less psychodynamic. Rather, they have simply been rewarded all their lives for thinking men have some special or God-given right to control women. A short temper and even violence are natural parts of manhood, they believe. Theirs is an attitude problem more than an emotional one.

It would trivialize the entire family violence problem simply to say that these men are victims. True, in many cases such men were the helpless victims of much abuse, but as adults they are driven by the same goals and needs as other men. That fact is the key to their transformation. As we shall show in chapter 6, they can learn and unlearn, undo and reconstitute attitudes and behavior. Nonviolent alternatives can be shown to achieve goals once clumsily pursued with violence and anger. They can learn, for the better, to appreciate women as equals and as persons who want to respond to men's needs if given the chance.

3
The Violent Woman

Myself and other units have made numerous calls over and over again to the J. household. Both Mr. and Mrs. have refused to move out of the house. This time he slapped her and bit her arm. She hit him in the face with her shoe. The whole situation appeared to be mutual combat.

—Police officer's official report
on a domestic disturbance call,
central Texas city

To most people women's violence against men, or wives' violence against their husbands, smacks of a grotesque joke. The idea of a physically smaller woman, rolling pin in hand, intimidating or battering her mate is fit material for burlesque skits. It conjures up images of amazons bullying passive, wimpish men. In fact, because of our Western patriarchal tradition, there is something that seems so absurd about women abusing men that until recently the entire subject of female violence has been almost ignored.

Yet violent women do exist. In our previous research we discovered that a number of battered men telephoned women's shelters every year seeking help as victims of violence. Police repeatedly told us stories of violent women they had personally encountered during domestic disturbance calls. And family counselors recalled cases where both clients in a couple had problems controlling their anger.

In this chapter we will explore the problem of women's violence. We want to know when and why it happens, how often, and what form it takes. We also want to distinguish instances of simple self-defense from those times when a woman is as violent or more violent than her husband or boyfriend. In so doing, we do not mean to take men's violence against women any less seriously. Admitting that some women can be violent in no way should obscure our concern about woman battering. Even in a family where the woman may be as violent as the man, their mutual hostilities do not cancel out each other. A problem still exists, but without understanding the woman's role, there will be no realistic solution. Before examining women's violence firsthand, however, we need to review briefly why so few investigators have broached the topic.

A Taboo Subject

There has been an almost conspiratorial silence about discussing women's violence toward men. When such violence has been self-defense, almost everyone agrees it is justified and looks no further. When a woman initiates a violent argument, say, with a slap to the man's face, but he finishes it by punching her unconscious, the natural reaction is to focus on the person who experienced the most injury. Again, most observers concern themselves with the woman as victim.

But there is a tendency to ignore or disclaim those cases where the woman is a violent person in her own right. There is little mystery about the general silence on this subject. A domineering and violent wife represents a parody of traditional patriarchal values. Men who are beaten fear they will be accused of being weak and unmasculine. Out of embarrassment they often do not seek help. The few men who called women's shelters in the Dallas–Fort Worth metroplex during our initial research in the early 1980s invariably were desperate, often telephoning from hospitals (such as the 6-foot 2-inch carpenter whose much smaller wife, a third-degree black belt in karate, had put him there with injuries for the fourth time) or feeling that they were at the point of ending their marriages. In one case, an Army sergeant could no longer deal with the private humiliation of his wife's violence toward him. Tears streaming down his face as his family said grace together one night before a meal, he quietly pulled a pistol from his belt, put the barrel in his mouth, and pulled the trigger. The daily contrast between his macho authoritarian parade-ground image with recruits and the reality of his being the frequent target of his domineering wife's physical abuse (in front of their children) became overwhelming.

Meanwhile, women's advocates who fought so long and hard to win recognition for women as victims of widespread male abuse fear that acknowledging that some women are perpetrators of violence (and therefore some men are victims) will trivialize the problem of woman battering. The notion that a woman could dominate or even brutalize a man also undermines the view that all women are victims, in some way, of male oppression. At a time when local and state government funding for battered women's shelters already is inadequate, there is resistance to seeing limited monies spent on programs dealing mostly with men. Having to compete for funding with programs that address women's violence is an even more appalling thought.

Even when a violent woman is known to exist, her case is dismissed as bizarre and not worth worrying about. If male abusers are not the sole problem in explaining family violence, the implication seems to be that the situation then becomes hopelessly complex.

Yet women's violence will not disappear because men who are injured by women usually are too ashamed to admit it or because women's advocates find that it does not fit into their movement's scheme of things. As understanding of family violence moves into the third systems phase we discussed previously and both men and women confront their problems as a couple in counseling, more and more professionals will have to come to grips with the reality of this problem.

In two of the three counseling programs we studied in Texas, a no-hitting rule had to be instituted for both partners during couples counseling sessions. Otherwise, violence could erupt even in relatively controlled situations. For instance, in one group session a husband and wife began arguing in front of the other clients over whether (of all things) they had had an argument the previous day. Incensed, the wife abruptly stood up and leaped onto her husband's lap, pinning his thighs to his chair with her knees as she put her hands around his throat and began to choke him. A male counselor had to pry her hands off and physically restrain her to make her stop.

In a society where girls are exposed to a cult of violence in much the same ways as boys, it would be surprising if men had a monopoly on frustration, hostility, and physical aggression. Drawing on a variety of sources, we explore the other side of the coin in family violence throughout the remainder of this chapter. Our goal is to shed light on the dynamics of violent families and relationships where women play a role other than that of passive victim.

How Often Are Women Violent?

There is no national clearinghouse or central government agency responsible for collecting information on spouse abuse. Thus we have no official figures for estimating how much family violence occurs across the country, much less any figures on women's violence against men. A few studies, however, have found evidence of female violence. One national survey of American families by sociologists Murray Straus, Richard Gelles, and Suzanne Steinmetz discovered just as much violence directed by women at men as vice versa (though the women usually were more severely injured).[1] One of these authors, Steinmetz, wrote a classic article titled "The Battered Husband Syndrome." She pointed out that husband beating is still a very camouflaged social problem because battered men are reluctant to come forward to seek help and because most researchers have been preoccupied with the problem of woman battering.[2] Although Steinmetz reminded readers that, blow for blow, larger, stronger men usually will do greater damage to smaller women than the reverse, she still received a good deal of criticism from women's advocates for even discussing the matter in print.

For some time police and criminologists have collected statistics that point to the existence of female violence. As early as 1956 criminologist Marvin E. Wolfgang reported evidence of husband homicides committed by wives (though Wolfgang also noted that the ratio of wives killed by husbands to husbands killed by wives was four to one—that is, women's violence was often not fatal).[3] More recently the *Texas Crime Victim Clearinghouse News* reported a study of police and sheriff's departments in the state and found that almost 10 percent of the victims of family violence were men.[4] Likewise, we examined one average month's computerized police reports (filed in the officers' own words) on almost four hundred domestic disturbance calls in one central Texas city and discovered that in 11 percent of the cases, women instigated the violence or were as violent as the men.

In 1985 sociologist Richard Breen studied 884 university students, both married and unmarried, and found that 18 percent of the men (compared to 14 percent of the women) reported having experienced violence by a romantic partner. Moreover, when he asked married male students about any specific types of female violence, they reported:

20 percent had wives who threw or broke household objects when angry;

23 percent had wives who punched, slapped, or kicked them;

30 percent had wives who pushed or shoved them in public or private;

9 percent said their wives had hit them with objects;

9 percent reported having received visible welts, cuts, bruises, and knots on heads, while 10 percent had sought aid at medical clinics, doctors' offices, or hospital emergency rooms as a result of spouses' violence;

14 percent said their wives had at least once threatened to kill either themselves or the men;

5 percent had called the police at least once because they felt in danger or they thought their family or friends might be in danger from their partners.[5]

It is possible, of course, that respondents in Breen's study exaggerated things such as pushes or shoves or interpreted an angry woman slamming a cupboard door as throwing things around. It is less likely, however, that they misinterpreted questions about specific injuries and obtaining medical assistance. What is most interesting is that few if any of these adult students (with an average age of 20) had arrest or assault records, and the vast majority of violent instances were what could be called moderate (shoving, slapping, and other nonlethal types). While the police seem to be seeing approximately one domestic disturbance call in ten involving serious female violence, Breen's more representative sample of law-abiding citizens reports several forms of moderate forms of female violence in two out of ten cases. This is consistent with what we already know from criminology about the official underreporting of assault and other criminal acts.

Thus there are reasonable indications that women are and can be violent toward men. According to crime statistics (which reflect more serious types of assault), women rather than men are more likely victims. Studies of the noncriminal population (such as that of Straus, Gelles, and Steinmetz), however, generally find roughly equal amounts of less severe violence between men and women, with men reporting higher rates of women's violence than popular stereotypes would suggest.

But the numbers cannot tell us the whole story. We do not know, for example, who starts fights in relationships or when the women are acting only in self-defense. The numbers leave us with an incomplete picture of women's violence, identifying it but not explaining it. To obtain a thorough understanding, we must supplement percentages and averages with a more indepth examination of the individual couples.

When Are Women Violent?

One can think of several possible situations in which a woman might be physically violent. For example, she might use force to protect herself. She might have trouble controlling her anger and lash out first in an argument at a man who also is prone to violence. Or she might have anger and violence tendencies but be living with a man who does not. In other words, a woman could be physically violent in self-defense, as the instigator of mutual violence, or as the sole perpetrator of violence in a given family.

To explore these three possibilities, we draw on a sample of forty-five couples from the Austin and Tyler counseling programs described in chapter 2 and in appendix A. For each couple we have information based on both the man's and woman's description of the violence before and after counseling as well as, in most cases, detailed counselors' notes and other assessments of the couple. In addition, we have one average month's narrative reports by police officers for forty-three domestic disturbance calls involving female violence in one central Texas city. Our intent is to describe women's violence in these situations. Having accomplished that, we will then be able to turn to the more important task of explaining why these women were violent.

Women's Violence in Self-Defense

Women's use of physical violence in self-defense might seem to need no explanation: They are instinctively trying to protect themselves from abusive men. Our inspection of police files turned up numerous cases where officers encountered husbands and boyfriends scratched, bit, cut, and slapped after women refused to submit passively to abuse. True, these women often were not successful in stopping the beatings, but at least they fought back. The most frequent weapons used were fingernails. The next most commonly used weapons were kitchen knives. A number of women used their teeth to bite men's limbs. Fingers were a particular injury point (especially when violent men tried to muffle the women's screams by placing hands over their mouths). Wrists, forearms, and even ear lobes also were bitten.

In other instances the women defended themselves with whatever items were handy when they were attacked: hot irons, kitchen utensils, furniture, even fireplace pokers. One police officer reported:

> [I was] dispatched to 4079 L Street in response to a domestic disturbance. Mr. and Mrs. Boone were present. Mr. Boone was bleeding from a cut to the left temple. The wound was sustained when the two had been arguing. Mr. Boone hit Mrs. Boone with a wrapped-up shirt. She retaliated with a cowboy boot to his head. Mr. Boone was extremely intoxicated at the time.

Some of the women's violence escalated beyond the men's first violent acts. For example, several men who slapped women were cut by spouses wielding butcher knives or buck knives. The fact that the men often were intoxicated meant that their reactions were slower, giving the women an additional advantage. In other cases, however, the women too had been drinking heavily, thus lowering their inhibitions. After cutting the men and seeing the blood, they occasionally panicked and called the police. One woman simply left her husband sitting in a pool of blood and fled into the night without even taking her preadolescent children with her. Suffice it to say that these women, out of fear and other emotions, sometimes combined with the effects of alcohol, did not make rational calculations as to what means of defense would equal the men's assaults. They simply fought back in desperation.

Once in a while abused women retaliate in the extreme, killing their mates. In chapter 1 we described one case where a woman accidentally killed her abusive husband, previously having found that pulling a knife made him retreat from abusing her. In *The Family Secret* we dealt explicitly with this subject from a legal standpoint: What were a woman's chances of winning acquittal in court if she chose the supremely violent act of killing an abusive man? The biggest obstacle for any jury, we concluded, was that for a woman regularly enduring abuse, no single instance seemed to justify the abuser's death on the grounds of self-defense. Only when the full history of the violent relationship could be told, and the psychology of ambivalence, fear, and dependence on the woman's part explained, could a jury see the act as justifiable self-defense.

None of the women in our current study killed their violent mates. And, similar to what many professionals working in the family violence field have observed, when these women did try to defend themselves against larger, angry men, they usually came out the losers. In almost every case we examined, women who tried to block punches, return slaps, and throw objects at men were more badly injured than the men. What is perhaps of more interest are cases we shall mention where women accepted (through bitter experience) the fact that openly attempting to defend themselves was futile but fought back more subtly for revenge.

Women as Instigators of Violence

There is a common saying among advocates of battered women to the effect that provocation does not mean justification. They mean that a woman's behavior, no matter how rude, insulting, or shrewish, can never be accepted as an excuse for a man to hit her. They usually do not have in mind that she might hit him first.

Women who instigate physically violent arguments appear to have the same handicap as many violent men when it comes to controlling their tempers. Verbal disagreements escalate in tone and decibels until the women strike out in frustration, and the men frequently respond in kind. For some women this is a regular pattern, as was the case for Karen and her husband Lyle. In the words of their counselor:

> The last assault occurred when Lyle came home drunk and they argued about his being late. Karen slapped him, and he broke some furniture, then pushed her around, banged her head against the wall, and slapped her several times. All his violence has occurred after he has been drinking (at least a six pack of beer a day when he is under stress). When arguments occur when he is sober, she will slap him and he will simply restrain her.

Many times when police arrive at such a domestic disturbance it is not clear just who is assailant and who is victim because each partner is angry, perhaps bruised or bloodied, and tentatively willing to file assault charges. One woman, Rebecca, wanted to file charges against her husband Ray, but the city's (female) assistant district attorney decided that Rebecca's own violence had spoiled the chances for successful prosecution. Ray had blackened Rebecca's eye (which police photographed for evidence), but prior to that she had accused her husband during an argument of having an affair with another woman. As she became more angry, Ray tried to leave, but Rebecca hid his car keys. In the ensuing shouting match she struck him on the arm, scratched his face, and snatched his glasses off his head and smashed them. Then he hit her.

By the standards of middle-class morality, such violence often occurs in appalling circumstances of insensitivity, lack of respect, and poor communication. For example, one such unsavory couple were Herman Balboa and his common-law partner Bernice. Bernice called the police, claiming Herman had punched her in the eye. Said the officer answering the call:

> I was unable to see any injury to her eye. I then spoke to Balboa, who stated that when he got home from work he asked her if she had made anything to eat. She stated, "Fuck you! If you want to eat, go back to Puerto Rico!" He then asked her if she was going to whore around all day.

According to Herman, he went up to their bedroom in disgust. Bernice followed and began hitting and scratching him. Only then did he hit her in return. A sullen Bernice would not talk to the officer about the incident, but Herman had deep scratch marks on the right side of his face.

Sometimes who gets defined as the victim and who finally is charged as the assailant may be only a matter of who called the police first and filed assault charges. Both partners may want to file charges, or neither may do so. One reason many men do not file charges is that they feel it would be unmanly or unchivalrous to go to the police for protection from a woman. For many men having to file charges and go through court procedures openly announces that they could not control what goes on within their own homes. It seems akin to cowardice. Hence they rarely file against abusive women.

In more than one police report we found that women assaulted husbands in front of police who had been called by neighbors or husbands to restore peace on the scene. If the police officer became physically involved in trying to stop the violence, then the odds were much better that an arrest would be made. On one call an officer found a couple who had begun arguing during a move out of their apartment. The officer attempted to break up the fight, but the wife refused to let go of her husband's hair. Finally the exasperated officer arrested her.

Some men ended up in the Austin counseling program after they had become physically violent trying to protect themselves from women's assaults. One man had attended a little league baseball game with his new wife and stepson, then took the family to a fast food restaurant to celebrate the victory. His jealous ex-wife entered and saw him with his new family. She walked over to their table in a rage and slapped him as he stood up, then turned to slap his new wife. "She can hit me but not my wife," he told a counselor. He caught her wrist and returned the slap. She filed charges.

In a similar instance where the man being counseled for violence was not the one who started fighting, a man had divorced his high-tempered wife. After being on her own for several months, she found herself broke and without rent money. He agreed to let her sleep on the couch in his apartment living room while she looked for a job. Unfortunately, he began returning home from work to find her making love to men she had picked up during the day. When they had it out over this new development, she picked up a wooden chair and began swinging it at him. She back him down a hallway toward his bedroom until he caught the chair and struck her. She filed charges. ("Why didn't you go into the bedroom and duck out a window?" a counselor asked him, hoping to make the instructive point that men can choose to walk away from such violent confrontations in the home. The male assailant replied, "Man, my apartment is on the fourth floor!")

Nor does the man always win because he is bigger. One couple in an Austin bar began to argue over their mutual jealousies of each other. Finally the man felt he had heard enough. He slapped his wife and turned his back on her. As he started to walk out, she picked up a long-necked beer bottle from the bar and smashed it over his head. When police arrived, he was taken away as the assailant and ended up in the Austin counseling program.

A woman we will call Billy Jean quintessentially represents many of these women who instigate violence:

Billy Jean was a 32-year-old woman who had been living with her boyfriend for about three years when she sought counseling for the violence in her relationship. She readily admitted that she started most of the violence. This violence had not been extreme—most of the time she slapped him or threw household objects at him, usually at his head. She admitted that she really wanted to hurt him when she was that angry. She said that although she had always had a hot temper, it had only been in recent months that she had become violent. In Billy Jean's case there had been several contributing factors to create strain in the relationship, including heavy alcohol use and the fact that her unemployed boyfriend was not trying hard enough to find a job.

Thus, although as many as one-third of the women considered here actually took the initiative in starting a violent quarrel with men, the men more often than not were the ones against whom assault charges were filed. In counseling many men mentioned this and resented having been labeled as the villain by the court. Later in this chapter we will look at violent couples as interacting units of hostility. Here we note that in filing assault charges, the women simply seemed to be further expressing their anger, either because the men would not let the women hit them any further or because the police broke up the confrontation before rage had run its course.

Women as Sole Perpetrators of Violence

In some cases women are the violent persons in their families. In the counseling programs we studied, these women were a minority: Only one in ten women matched this description. In the police reports on domestic disturbance calls, however, such women made up almost one-third of the cases.

One question that immediately comes to mind when the subject of violent women living with nonviolent men arises is "What kind of men are these?" Our own experience is that most people expect them to be effeminate or frail and nonassertive. Wimps, pussies, and closet fags are terms we have heard.

In fact, this is rarely the case. Many times the men have tried unsuccessfully to extricate themselves from arguments with women or were hit when their guard was down. One police officer reported violence against a man who had gone to his girlfriend's house and soon found himself in an argument. As her temper and voice rose together, he thought it best to leave. When he headed out the back door onto the carport, she hurled a glass that shattered against the back of his head. He was one of a literal handful of men who pressed assault charges. On another domestic disturbance call police arrived to find a man sitting on his front porch with blood pouring from his nose. He had been asleep after working the late shift at a nearby factory. That morning his ex-girlfriend (with whom he had recently broken up) came to his house and persuaded his mother to let her into the house. She immediately went to his bedroom. According to the mother, who tried unsuccessfully to restrain her, the ex-girlfriend "began to scream and then began hitting" the sleeping man. As he rose off his pillow, she grabbed him by the hair and drove her knee full into his face. Neighbors called the police, who took him to the hospital. No arrest was made.

Sometimes a woman's violence is part of the dogged pursuit of a man, which mirrors the domination (and possible emotional dependence) of violent men. One counselor told the following story illustrating such persistence:

Jerry is a 34-year-old construction contractor who recently went to court for the tenth time on an assault charge brought against him by his ex-wife. On each charge he has pleaded not guilty, and each time his wife has failed to show up at the trial, therefore the charges against him have been dropped. But each time nevertheless he has had to hire a lawyer, taken time off from his job, and spent many hours trying to explain to his current girlfriend that he has not been violent against his ex-wife. He says his girlfriend (with whom he has never been violent) is now threatening to leave him if this goes on much longer. He no longer knows what to do. He has been to the police department and has been told that there is nothing they can do. She can file whatever charges against him she wants, and then it is up to the courts to decide whether he is guilty or not. He has been told to hire a lawyer.

He has been divorced from his wife for about a year and a half. It was a bitter divorce with a child custody case that he won. His ex-wife told him repeatedly that she would make life miserable for him and eventually would get the children from him. Jerry once told the counselor when speaking about her, "You want to see violence? I'll show you violence!" He showed a recent cut on his forearm "This is what she did the last time she got angry with me." When the counselor asked why he did not file charges against her, Jerry flatly said that he was a man and that he would not ever call the police on a woman. His lawyer told him that there is little he can do except file a civil suit against her since she most recently has taken to harassing him at work. She also has promised to get him fired from his job and many times has shown up at job sites screaming accusations at him and telling his co-workers how he has beaten her.

Other times the violence transparently reveals motives of revenge:

Ken was a 28-year-old man who appeared in court on an assault charge brought against him by his former live-in girlfriend. He pleaded not guilty and flatly denied ever having been violent with her. He said he decided to move out of this relationship because she had an uncontrolled drinking problem, became violent whenever she drank to excess, and refused to seek any kind of help. Once he had to call the police when he moved out because she blocked the doorway and would attack him when he tried to leave. When the police arrived, he was able to remove his belongings.

Since leaving he had to move twice because she came to his apartment and, if he refused to let her in, would yell threats, break windows, and scream until neighbors called the police. About a month ago she came to his new apartment and talked a new roommate of his into letting her into the apartment while he was sleeping. She came into his room and stabbed at his groin with a pair of scissors, puncturing his scrotum. He had to be hospitalized after being taken to a hospital emergency room. Since that time he has had all four of his car tires slashed. Yet Ken refused to file any kind of charges against her, or take out peace bonds or any protective orders, because she is a woman.

There are common stress elements in the lives of both men and women who are the sole perpetrators of violence in relationships: financial problems, with both or either of the partners out of work; alcohol abuse; sexual frustration; and feelings that the other person must be made to act more appropriately (according to whatever standards the perpetrator holds). The final case of Carolyn demonstrates the same sort of dependence and fears that characterize violent men:

Carolyn was a 32-year-old mental health professional who was periodically violent with a live-in boyfriend for two years. She admitted throwing garbage at him, hitting him with her fists, and attacking him with a broom handle. Her boyfriend was much bigger than she and never responded with violence to these assaults. He usually left the house for a while or restrained her and took away the object she was trying to use on him. She said that she became violent when she was frustrated in trying to communicate with him and could not explain what she wanted him to do. She felt helpless and the need to make him respond to her. She also confessed that she knew the relationship was alive [her word] when they argued intensely enough to arouse violence. She greatly feared that he would take her for granted and that the relationship would become stagnant. Eventually she feared she would lose her identity as an individual.

These vignettes and samples of women's violence suggest some intriguing parallels with men's violence. Women may be more likely than men to use kitchen utensils or sewing scissors when they commit assault, but their frustrations, motives, and lack of control over these feelings predictably resemble men's. Having established that women can indeed be every bit as violent as men, we now consider why some women seem to be violent.

Why Are Women Violent?

No area of family violence studies is more exploratory than the problem of women's violence for reasons we have already mentioned. The following profile of violent women, therefore, is an approximation, undoubtedly to be reshaped by later research.

Everything we have found points to parallel processes that lead women and men to become violent. In fact, what we know of these women's backgrounds as well as their adult lives closely mirrors those of violent men. This conclusion is a mixed blessing. On the one hand, it means that we will not need to create two separate therapies or different sets of counseling approaches. Logically, if violence emerges for the same reasons, then it can be stopped in the same way. On the other hand, this conclusion offers a sad indictment of the cult of violence so prevalent in our society. It appears to contaminate everyone, regardless of gender.

We have distilled the factors underlying women's violence to four crucial dimensions: reverse sexism, the inheritance of violence, lack of social skills, and exposure to stressors. They obviously are similar to those discussed in relation to men and help place women's violence in the context of the violent home.

Reverse Sexism

Just as many men, reared in patriarchal tradition and supported by macho ideas in modern culture, feel that control of a relationship is their right and violence their prerogative, so many women are exposed to a flip side of that tradition. Under certain circumstances it is considered all right for a woman to slap a man (particularly if he gets fresh with her or insults her). The proverbial skillet-over-the-head routine, or the stereotype of an angry matronly housewife carrying a rolling pin like a menacing battle-ax, also are elements of this flip side. The logic goes something like this:

> Men are bigger and stronger than women.
>
> Thus men have a special responsibility to be protective and morally restrained toward women and treat them like ladies. Sometimes men misbehave so that women are justified in physically slapping or threatening them to correct their actions.
>
> Because of their physical advantage in an actual fight, men are supposed to accept the slap without resistance as a reminder of their responsibility. To retaliate in kind would be unfair.

Conditioned by such reverse sexist expectations, we argue, many women become involved in heated domestic combat that frequently is not restrained by any rules. Some women do not mean to instigate an exchange of blows with mates but end up doing just that. Other women, because of frustration and hostility, seem to forget this logic and make a slap the prelude to more serious aggression by men.

The Inheritance of Violence

The most common explanation offered for why men batter has been the generational transfer hypothesis. The idea behind generational transfer is that little boys see violence in the home between their parents so it becomes associated with strong emotions such as love, fear, security, and dependence. They learn that it is a practical, appropriate way for men to treat and control women. And often they are on the receiving end of parental violence, perhaps even physical or sexual abuse. Our own past research, as well as studies by others, has shown this to be generally true of many violent men.[6]

The reverse effect of generational transfer used to be applied to battered women—that is, women learned from watching their mothers being beaten (and also from being hit themselves) to be passive victims. They were to accept violence from a stronger man who also delivered affection and companionship as right and normal. In recent years research on battered women has largely thrown out this part of the generational transfer hypothesis. We now have a much clearer idea of why many women do not leave a relationship when it starts becoming violent, and the reasons usually do not include that the woman thinks the violence is normal or unexceptional.[7]

Yet experiencing violence in the childhood home does affect women, not in teaching them to be victims but in showing them when to use violence themselves. In other words, the learning process of generational transfer works the same for both sexes. In talking with men about their in-laws and interviewing women about their childhood home lives, counselors frequently found that violent women came from violent families and often experienced child abuse. Just as these conditions produce emotionally dependent men feeling that they are inadequate and need to control the immediate world around them, so the same conditions produce dependent women with low self-esteem and hostility.

Not every violent woman fits such a profile or is a product of the generational transfer, or inheritance, of family violence. Certainly it does not explain the actions of women who act in self-defense. It does, however, account for most, if not all, of the perpetrators and most of the instigators. Sometimes women are exposed to several forms of abuse, such as witnessing it between parents and then being sexually abused by fathers, uncles, or other male relatives. Many in counseling had been emotionally ignored by abusive fathers except when the fathers were drunk or annoyed. The majority had elements of frustration, dependence, and hostility interwoven into their personalities early in life.

This package of hostility and dependence worked its way out in the jealousy and suspicion of many women that their husbands or boyfriends were unfaithful. In sociologist Richard Breen's study of university students mentioned earlier, he found that men with violent wives reported that the wives tended to monitor the husbands' time closely and make them account for every minute spent when running errands or visiting friends. They discouraged men from having friendships with other women as well as with other men and were overly critical of their husbands' manners and appearances, even ridiculing them in public. Anger sometimes was expressed by emotional coldness followed by abrupt Jekyll and Hyde mood changes to loud and abusive behavior.

Anyone familiar with battered women's descriptions of abusive men will recognize a classic pattern of domination, possessiveness, emotional dependence, and insecurity. We also found this pattern in the families of men who went through the Austin diversion program. A sample of sixty-seven men filled out a questionnaire about possible domineering and violent behavior by their wives or girlfriends. The questionnaire was one the Center for Social Research Abuse Index developed for interviewing abused women about their husbands and estimating the level of violence faced.[8] The questions dealt with a range of violent actions as well as domineering, possessive ones (such as constantly monitoring the mate's time and discouraging outside friendships).

We knew that the majority of violent men initially minimized or rationalized their own violence when first entering counseling and were irrefutably confronted with their problem. Therefore we had every reason to expect exaggeration of the women's possessiveness and violence as the men tried to excuse what they had done. Yet not all men minimize or rationalize. For example, we know independently of what the men told us that many of their parents were violent. The results of the questionnaire told basically the same story as Breen's study:

Two-thirds reported that their mates regularly went through their pockets and billfolds, not so much looking for money as for telephone numbers of possible girlfriends.

Three-fourths said the women closely clocked them while they were outside the home.

One-third of the women tried to censor the men's telephone calls and other communications with family and friends.

Two-thirds said the women withdrew sex as punishment when they resisted being monitored or misbehaved somehow.

The men also reported women's physical violence. Two-thirds said the women threw things at them or smashed objects. While half had been threatened physically (the majority with being killed), half the men had been punched or kicked. There undoubtedly is distortion at work in these reports but we know from the previously documented case reports that women's violence cannot be dismissed as sheer rationalization.

Lack of Social Skills

As the examples of women's violence have made clear, many of these women do not have the ability to control their anger. They also lack the skills to deal with problems that arise in intimate relationships with men. At the same time many women are products of traditional cultural values that prize passive female behavior. They have little or no experience in taking the initiative to express their own needs and opinions to men yet understandably are pressured to communicate in some way. They have never learned to negotiate openly as equals with their partners. Ironically, violence becomes the end result of the lack of effective communication skills.

Knowing no alternatives, they become frustrated and try violence as a means to settle disagreements in the same way that men do. Combine the handicap of poor communication skills with a willingness to turn frustrations into rage, and then add a man with similar problems. The results are now filling our family courts and women's shelters.

Exposure to Stressors

Stressors are those points in every person's life that make it more difficult. Some stressors are minor irritants, like cat fights outside a bedroom window at night or traffic jams. Other stressors are more important: job insecurity and unemployment, sexual impotence or frigidity, jealousy, alcoholism, and drug abuse. All these problems are evident in the lives of both violent men and women. Stressors do not cause the violence but instead become the bases of arguments and disagreements between men and women. As we have seen, many men and women cannot find nonviolent ways to deal with them. The mounting tension that results is analogous to steam in a boiler with no safety valve.

Are modern women becoming more violent than previous generations of women, or are we simply finding violent women because our post–World War II society finally has recognized all family assaults as a social problem? We have no way of knowing for sure, but many of the stressors in the lives of these women, such as economic factors, are things either beyond their immediate control or beyond any individual's control. Nothing we have seen of modern technological society suggests that such stressors will decrease in the future. On the contrary, most likely they will increase.

Violent Women and Violent Men

John Patrick, director of counseling at the Tyler Family Preservation Project, believes from his experience that in some families an atmosphere of violence comes to exist that draws all members of the family into it one way or another. In many ways it becomes symbiotic between man and woman— that is, each person's violence, or reaction to violence, depends on the other's and may even contribute to it. In his counseling experience Patrick feels that many of the couples he interviews have mutual hostility and resentment against the world. "They find each other, somehow," he explained. "They form a bond or a symbiosis so that it's 'Us against the world.' " The men and women often come from the same backgrounds, such as having violent home lives with one or both parents emotionally indifferent to them. As a result each partner brings the same weaknesses to adult relationships: emotional dependence, childlike insecurity, and a generally low self-image. That is why, Patrick believes, these persons attract each other. They form a partnership of mutual dependence, shoring up each other's weaknesses and isolating each other from a world they believe is cruel and stress-laden. To outsiders their violence may seem to be a good reason for one or the other to leave or file for divorce. On closer analysis, however, the violence is simply a piece of the larger psychology of mutual need.

Patrick believes that far from being sociopaths or emotionally callous, such persons are very sensitive. The problem is that they have trouble interpreting feelings of hurt or need, much less expressing them to their partners. They do experience stress from these feelings, however, which translates into anger. And anger at least is something both partners understand. Many of the men in the Tyler program felt that they were abandoned or neglected as boys (several men who had been sodomized or fondled by male relatives very reluctantly talked about these events, as if they feared they would be branded queer) and expected women to make up for those hurts. Their adult needs, when frustrated or slighted, reactivated that childhood sense of abandonment and led them to overreact with rage and violence. The same appears to be the case with women.

Recently John Patrick, along with his counseling colleague Carol Mantooth and University of Texas psychologist Robert Geffner, presented a paper to the American Psychological Association that put this interpretation to the test.[9] They administered questionnaires to thirty-seven couples (men and women) in which at least one member was physically violent. They used standardized questions to measure, among other things, the client's assertiveness, level of self-esteem, and hostility. What they found indicates that "likes" do attract "likes" in many instances, as both male and female clients tended to have lower than normal levels of self-esteem. More importantly, these clients tended to be beyond the normal ranges of hostility and dominance/submission.

The large amount of hostility is a critical factor in understanding what patterns violence takes in such homes. One woman, Margaret, had been violent toward other women before she married Peter. A woman with low self-esteem, Margaret sometimes engaged in apparently juvenile, annoying acts to gain attention from others. Violence was one such means. Peter, however, was too big and hostile himself for her to beat him up, yet she persisted in doing things that to an outsider looked suspiciously as if she was going out of her way to provoke his temper. A typical attention-getting device was to turn up the sound on the car radio to an obnoxiously blaring level when a song Peter liked was played. The fact that this ploy frequently backfired did not keep her from repeating it.

Other women channel their hostility more subtly. One middle-aged man, married to the same woman for twenty years, was a church leader and upstanding civic figure. He was periodically abusive to his wife. After finding that she was physically no match for him, the woman engaged in a deliberate sabotage of his lifestyle as a way of hitting back. She told counselors how for years she had purposely misironed her husband's shirts and overcooked or undercooked his meals. She laughed as she revealed that she always made sure she served him food on cracked plates, gave him the bent fork or chipped drinking glass, and even made it a point to break the yokes in his eggs no matter how he wanted them cooked. Her revenge was that he never knew.

Other women, like Margaret, are more direct. They want to share their hostility and resentment through insults and criticism that goad their mate. It is their ineffective and even pathetic way to try to generate the very emotional response that their husbands and boyfriends also desperately want but are incapable of giving.

A Final Word

Most of this chapter has dealt with women's violence, but it should be clear that we will never really make progress in resolving family violence if we do not consider the family as the unit to be helped. Until recently spouse abuse has been synonymous with woman battering. Now we know things are not always so one-sided. The worst fears of feminist Susan Schechter cited in chapter 1 have been realized: The professionals and the researchers are re-defining the problem as more than simply men's violence against women.

The implications are obvious. Agencies and counselors must adopt a much broader agenda than treating battered women's injuries or men's hostilities. Society's vision of violence must be thoroughly reformulated. While this new shift in focus reveals family violence to be a complicated issue doing away with more convenient black and white thinking on the subject, it also moves us closer to the final goal for all concerned persons: a realistic and effective way of stopping violence between men and women.

Part II
The Culture of Violence

Feminist writers have made an invaluable contribution by critically pointing out the various ways that culture, both subtly and not so subtly, reinforces sexist patriarchal norms, which encourage and rationalize abuse of women. The parts played by specific institutional areas of American culture, however, have not always received enough attention. Here we probe the influence of two important institutions that touch the lives of enormous numbers of Americans: the military and the church.

All branches of the military are acutely aware that violence within many military families is a significant problem. Its extent and severity have not been publicized, however, and comparisons with civilian family violence have never before been attempted. Despite the military's reluctance to provide details, we did obtain data on military families experiencing violence. Chapter 4 examines violence in these families, places it relative to known civilian levels, and highlights the unique features of military life that make family violence such a serious problem.

In chapter 5 we look at how religion encourages and discourages violence in a subsample of families from our larger study. It is a truism that almost any point of view can find some verse in the Bible to justify it. Certainly this is the case for men abusing women, but as we argue, it need not be that way.

4
Family Violence in the Military

> If the army wanted you to have a wife, they would have issued you one.
>
> —Old military saying

S
ince World War II the U.S. military establishment has changed as much as any other institution in our society. This is particularly true when we consider the number of active military personnel who are married. From 1953 to 1974, for example, the number of married service-men rose 48 percent, with the Army seeing the greatest increase. Currently almost 60 percent of active duty personnel in all branches of the service are married, many of them men who are 30 years of age or younger.[1]

Like their civilian counterparts, U.S. military families have experienced violence. How much violence is not exactly known. Yet all signs indicate that if widespread drug abuse and poor morale were the military's critical personnel problems of the 1970s, then violence within military families is its problem of the 1980s. Recognition of this problem by military officials and scholars is remarkably recent. Consider the following:

1979 The Navy's Bureau of Medicine and Surgery issued a directive for treatment of child abuse, rape, and spouse abuse at Navy hospitals. The Army and Air Force soon followed suit.

1981 In March more than 120 military and civilian social workers, counselors, doctors and nurses, clergy, lawyers, and battered women's advocates attended the first national conference ever held on violence in military families. The conference was sponsored by, among other groups, the Center for Women Policy Studies in Washington, D.C., and ad-dressed the concern of one speaker, Lieutenant General M. Colloer Ross, who stated: "Any threat to the military family is a threat to the military organization and our country's defense." In this light, he urged those attending to "pay serious attention to the problem of spouse abuse in military families because family problems can critically affect a soldier's performance."[2]

1981 A Department of Defense directive signed by Deputy Secretary of Defense Frank Carlucci mandated that each branch of the armed services develop programs for families experiencing child abuse and wife battering. Congress appropriated $5 million to develop and implement these new family advocacy programs.

1982 The Army established a Family Liaison Office in the Pentagon. One of its concerns is family violence. Likewise, the Navy started Family Service Centers, staffed by both military and civilian counselors, which are to be points of contact for people with problems such as family violence. By 1982 it had set up twenty-two centers. Its proclaimed goal is to have such centers located on all major shore bases with at least one thousand active duty personnel or five hundred families. The Air Force, meanwhile, intends to place similar Family Support Centers on every existing Air Force base.

1985 The March issue of the widely distributed *Family, The Magazine for Military Wives* (a sort of military version of *Redbook*) contained a frank article titled "10 Myths About Spouse Abuse" and offered women addresses where they could write for more information.

With the exception of one study of eighty military men conducted by psychologist Peter H. Neidig and his associates, however, we could find no article, book, or source that presented anything more than generalities about the problem. No one seemed to be generating systematic profiles of violent military men or collecting the other forms of information that we now have for violent civilians. Not even any statistics on the number of military men arrested or counseled for spouse abuse were available to the public.

Our own efforts to obtain such figures met with bureaucratic runa-rounds from military public relations personnel, polite but dead-end thank-yous-for-your-interest, or unanswered telephone calls and letters. Social scientists under contract with the military assured us that the information could be tallied but that access to it and permission to publish it were strictly controlled.

In part, this gap in our overall understanding of a family problem can be explained by the professional interests of those running these programs. Typically they are counselors and clinicians with neither the time nor the interest in assembling numbers from their case files. One sociologist who has researched the military family for many years wrote us:

> The specific field of family abuse . . . has received relatively little attention from the research community other than clinical studies. This, I suspect, is the major reason for the problems you've had in getting data. . . . However, I have seen no statistics on the incidence of family abuse in the military, and I doubt that the files of installation provost marshals and medical

authorities are in a form that would lend themselves to producing such statistics with any facility.[3]

There appears to be an additional reason why meaningful published research on family violence within the armed forces community has been so hard to come by. No one who has dealt with any branch of the military can deny its overall sensitivity to bad press and critical publicity. The military cannot be faulted simply because some of its families share an embarrassing problem in common with their civilian counterparts. Yet an institution totally supported by an enormous amount of tax dollars ought to be accountable to general citizens when a widespread problem affects its personnel. And that leads to this second reason for the military not freely offering statistics of details on the incidence of military family violence. As we shall show in our examination of several hundred military families, the severity of the violence committed there makes the usual patterns of violence in civilian families pale by comparison.

The Unique Context of Military Family Violence

Any society or organization places responsibilities, limitations, and stresses on members that are unique. Thus it is no surprise that the men and women of military families manage their lives quite differently from civilians.

Male Soldiers

From basic training to the everyday operating assumption of the career military man, male soldiers come to accept the military as a separate world within American society. Initially, all civilian statuses are disparaged. Isolation of soldiers from civilian culture, creating a we-they way for them to view their former friends and contacts, is demanded. Soldiers learn to be evaluated and judged less as individuals and more as parts of units. In particular, men must deal not only with stresses of all kinds (both psychological and physical) but also with a heavy emphasis on the masculinity and aggressiveness that research on civilians has found to be an important component of male violence toward women.[4]

This macho aspect of military education that men encounter when they first enter the military (and one that is continually reinforced as they pursue military careers, whether in combat readiness assignments or in desk jobs) is what sociologist Morris Janowitz, in his classic *The Professional Soldier,* called the fighter spirit. Says Janowitz, "The fighter spirit is not easily defined: it is based on a psychological motive, which drives a man to seek success in combat, regardless of his personal safety."[5]

Besides the warrior ethic, which is still alive and well in the high-tech peacetime military of the 1980s, another important element unique to the military institution is the extent to which it touches all aspects of a soldier's life. There is no simple line drawn between military business and family affairs. Indeed, what goes on within the walls of a man's home, if it becomes known elsewhere, reflects on his qualities as a soldier and may affect the man's chances for promotion.

In *Spouse Abuse—A Treatment Program for Couples,* Peter H. Neidig and Dale H. Friedman, who have worked extensively with military families, write:

> The regimentation and lack of privacy found in the military community, and particularly in military housing, often result in intrusions by authorities into areas of family life beyond what is found in the civilian community. Men may be called on to control their wives and children or be held directly responsible for their families' conduct. This dictate strongly suggests that the authoritarian model of the work place should also be applied to home. . . . However, this same model creates considerable conflict when it is attempted within the family . . . [as] the prevailing ethic in military communities of self-sufficiency and machismo reinforces the belief that any-one who experiences problems is not manly and should be weeded out. This belief tends to isolate those who are experiencing problems and makes it difficult for them to admit, even to their family or friends, that they are in trouble.[6]

This often has been the case with incidents of family violence. Soldiers who have the same problems of controlling anger, poor communication abilities, and exposure to sexist stereotypes as civilian men find that such factors significantly affect their jobs and careers. Alongside the pervading martial atmosphere of military life and concerns for discipline and control is a bureaucratic organization in the shape of a pyramid with lines of authority flowing from the apex downward to the base. As soldiers who must be (in theory at least) deployable for whatever purpose suits their superiors, military men find that the pyramid's authority extends into their intimate lives even if they do not wish to manage families by the military model. Thus it is no accident that earlier in this century, when the various military branches were experiencing tensions caused by a growing number of married men in the ranks, the expression arose: "If the army wanted you to have a wife, they would have issued you one."

Military Wives

The military wife is a fairly recent phenomenon, at least as far as official recognition of her presence and needs is concerned. In the past she (along with the children) was regarded simply as a dependent, akin to baggage that must be gathered up and moved with the soldier when he was ordered to his new assigned duty or stored at home while he was away. Since World War II the situation for military wives has improved considerably, but the twin problems of the isolation of military families from civilian society and the military's slowness to recognize the wives' situation inspired the use of the postwar phrase *khaki ghetto*.[7]

Most authors writing about the military family have dealt with the strains caused by frequent moving, inadequate pay and housing allowances, problems associated with intercultural and interracial marriages, separation of the soldier from his wife and children (so that sometimes the family becomes matricentric—that is, the wife ends up in what resembles a single-parent family), and even the high rates of alcoholism among military wives brought on by loneliness and other pressures.[8] Much also has been written about the important role the military wife plays in her husband's career. While the military services until recent years were not terribly responsive to the problems of soldiers' families, they were quick to consider those families part of the pyramid of authority in which they could expect obedience. Wives as well as soldiers regularly were lectured by senior military personnel on their duties.[9]

A good deal has changed in the past several decades, mainly because no branch of the military can afford to ignore the large (sometimes majority) number of active duty personnel who are married. The military now realizes that there is a direct relationship between a strong home life and a soldier's doing an effective job while on duty. Military literature now officially recognizes and endorses the family's support in a soldier's career, and women are encouraged to think of themselves as sharing more than a little in their husbands' achievements. One advertisement in a recent issue of *Family* (the magazine distributed to military families) showed a beaming young woman looking on as her uniformed husband received a decoration or promotion. The caption read: "Think of it this way. When your husband moves up so do you." The ad emphasized the benefits she and her family would enjoy from the husband's promotion, ending with the slogan: "Navy Wife. It's the toughest job in the Navy."

In fact, the wife's investment in her husband's career becomes especially important for officers' wives, and they are subjected to many pressures to become career assets for their husbands. M. Duncan Stanton described this role:

> The socialization of an Army officer's wife follows quite closely to that of the ambassador's wife. As in embassy service, the senior officers' wives acquaint the newcomer with the hazards of her role. She is told what her days as an officer's helpmate should be like and that if she is to uphold the military traditions and be a complement to her husband officer, military considerations should have priority over personal interests, friends, and

nonmilitary loyalties. Written guidebooks and pamphlets list specific duties and obligations that she is to assume and strongly suggest her involvement with other officers' wives in their organizations.[10]

In fact, Stanton tells of one secretary of the Army during the 1970s who wrote that a senior officer under consideration for promotion should be rated negatively if his wife was a potential embarrassment to the military.

The military wife's heavy investment in her husband's career, and the role expected of her, pose special problems if he becomes physically abusive toward her. Although programs now exist to counsel violent men and aid women and children, from ordering him to live apart in barracks while receiving counseling to helping her move out, a woman clearly jeopardizes her husband's chances for advancement, particularly in a peacetime military, if she seeks help for his problem. One important reason is the lack of confidentiality that operates in the armed forces. Every communication between a serviceman and a doctor, mental health professional, social worker, lawyer, or anyone else (except a chaplin) becomes part of his permanent file that may be inspected at any time by the man's commander. Likewise, if the wife turns to medical or social services provided by the military, that information also becomes part of the ongoing record.

As a result, it is fair to assume several things about the known cases of military family violence, including those we will discuss in the following pages. First, most of these women took seriously the notion that they had a special responsibility as military wives. Second, virtually all were aware of the specific benefits they and their families would enjoy as their husbands' careers progressed. This meant that leaving their homes or putting the men on report (that is, calling military or civilian police or filing assault charges) would have jeopardized their own future security. Third and last, given all these reasons not to call attention to violence in the family, there is good reason to think that the cases of military family violence so far discovered represent only the tip of an iceberg proportionately much larger than its civilian counterpart.

The Study Site

Initially we were stymied by a lack of meaningful cooperation from military personnel whom we had contacted. We were courteously sent descriptions of counseling programs for wife-abusing soldiers and sailors around the country. No one could or would, however, provide particulars on the numbers of men involved or details on violent incidences. The "word" we repeatedly received was that the military was addressing the family violence problem and that we should be content to know that.

Because it appeared that information on family violence was not going to be forthcoming from such official sources, in the spring of 1984 we decided to find our own cases and generate our own trends. Thus we obtained information on 356 cases of spouse abuse from a women's shelter in a north-central Texas community adjacent to Fort Hood, the largest U.S. Army land base in the United States. Of those cases, covering the years 1982–1984, 231 involved the families of active duty soldiers and will be our focus here.

Each case contained data collected by a shelter staff person on a seven-page document during interviews with female clients soon after they came to the shelter. This information included basic descriptive demographic information (such as race, formal education, income, and number of children) for both the women and their husbands or boyfriends as well as details about past and recent violent episodes and the men's and women's reactions after such incidences.[11]

Fort Hood, Texas, is the training site of approximately 45,000 troops (mostly infantry and cavalry) from around the country. Its commanding lieutenant general is a former West Point commandant, a Vietnam veteran, and a man genuinely concerned about the problem of spouse abuse in Army families. During the years covered by our study, the Army established a contract with the community's women's shelter to provide the latter $30 per Army wife and an additional $30 per child for each day these dependents remained at the shelter as a result of spouse abuse. Because of the high turnover of soldiers stationed at Fort Hood, their broad variety of geographic backgrounds before being assigned there, and the fact that this shelter (unlike many) had the financial means to accommodate virtually all military wives who contacted it for help, this sample of battered women gives us an excellent opportunity to look at the relatively unpublicized military family violence problem.

In addition, it will be helpful in assessing these 231 military cases to compare them with a known sample of civilian cases involving men who were never exposed to military training and who did not reside in a community dominated by a military presence as large as Fort Hood. We have such cases from our earlier study of shelter residents in the Dallas–Fort Worth metroplex (reported in *The Family Secret*). Women from these families were interviewed by the same procedure as the women from military families, thus we will include them in this analysis. Later we will show good reason for comparing military families with civilians outside the community adjacent to Fort Hood rather than with civilian families from that same community.

The Findings

Before assessing violence in the military family, we will describe the batterers, their victims, and the violent incidences that prompted women to go to the shelter adjacent to Fort Hood.

Male Batterers and Their Victims

The most striking feature of the soldiers who literally drove their wives out of their homes is that they were virtually all enlisted men. Officers' wives were nearly nonexistent among the 236 women from military families. Does this mean that wife abuse is exclusively a problem of men in the lower ranks? Far from it. Rather, the absence of officers' wives in our study reflects several realities about the military's treatment of violent men.

First, the truth is that the officer corps takes care of its own. Many of these men who have served together, gone through training together, or who evaluate each other are reluctant to report their friends and colleagues. Some may not even consider woman battering a problem worth reporting. Moreover, careers can be made or broken by damaging personal information placed in their service files. Thus wife-beating officers were a rare species in the military program at Fort Hood, just as their wives rarely came to the community's women's shelter.

This fact was confirmed during a conversation with the captain psychologist who ran Fort Hood's military program. He told us, "During the course of one full year I would estimate that I counsel about five hundred men who have been reported to me for abusing women or children."

One of us asked, "On a military base of 45,000 troops, do you think that number gives an accurate picture of spouse abuse?"

"No," the captain replied, "It's likely an underestimate."

"What percentage of those cases involved officers?" we asked.

"Officers don't have this problem," the captain replied with a deadpan expression.

One of us asked him to repeat that statement.

The captain did, this time with a wink. Officers frequently were able to keep themselves from receiving official censure, he said, and thereby avoid the pressures to enter counseling. Besides fellow officers' covering up such violence, another reason for the scarcity of officers' wives in shelters is the wives' belief (strongly reinforced by every branch of the military) that his career—and ultimately her fate—are tied to his clean record. Such a woman has a far greater investment, both in terms of finances and prestige, in keeping blemishes such as domestic assault off his service record. (An added factor at this particular shelter was that a number of officers' wives served either on the board of directors or on the staff, further erasing hope of discretion and anonymity.)

Age. This modern volunteer army in no way represents a cross-section of American society. This can be seen clearly in the ages of the military batterers shown in table 4–1. The average age of military wife beaters was a youthful 25 years compared to 31 years for the civilian men. The same pattern generally was true for the victims, as their ages tended to resemble their husbands'. Among the 236 military families, however, we found 72 marriages (or about one-third) where the wife was older than the husband. This is unusual, not only compared to our civilian subsample (where the man usually was the same age or a few years older than his wife) but also compared to customs in our society.

To our knowledge, none of the published literature on military family violence—which is almost always nonstatistical—has ever mentioned such a finding. Moreover, we found that the frequency and severity of the violence committed was higher for those couples than for the remaining families in which men were older than their wives. We can suggest several possible reasons. One may be that in couples where the wife was older, she felt or acted more independently than her husband preferred. (Given that many of battering men are domineering as well, this explanation is highly plausible.) Another reason might be that older women possessed greater communication skills than their younger husbands, a further frustrating factor for angry men. There is no question, however, that couples with such age disparities not only go against the grain of American culture but also are potentially more incompatible.

Education. In recent years it has been the policy of all branches of the military to accept only volunteers with a high school education or its equivalent.

Table 4–1
Frequency Distribution of Military and Civilian Batterers by Age

	Active Military		Civilians	
Age	N	%	N	%
17–19	15	7.1	7	2.7
20–24	98	46.2	55	21.1
25–29	63	29.7	81	31.1
30–34	28	10.9	57	21.8
35–39	9	4.3	28	10.7
40–44	2	0.9	16	6.1
45–49	0	0.0	7	2.7
50+	2	0.9	10	3.8
Total[a]	217	100.0	261	100.0

[a]Totals vary as not all respondents answered this question.

Thus members of our military sample are on the average better educated than members of the civilian samples (table 4–2). Only one-fifth of the soldiers had less than a high school education compared to well over half of the civilians. Conversely, two-thirds of the soldiers had a high school education compared to only one-third of the civilians. Certainly lack of education among peacetime Army volunteers cannot be used to explain their violence.

Race and Ethnicity. A third factor that makes our sample of military batterers different from the civilian sample is the high percentage of minorities in the former group (table 4–3). While the majority of civilian batterers were white, slightly more than half the soldiers were black, a little less than one-third were white, and one in five were Hispanic.

This comes as no surprise, as the U.S. military has attracted many minorities since World War II. (These servicemen see the military as an avenue for career mobility and job security at a time when economic recession and the effects of discrimination still linger.) A related fact of interest also emerged. One in five of the troubled military marriages (or 52 out of 236 families) were interracial and/or intercultural. For example, fifteen white women were

Table 4–2
Frequency Distribution of Military and Civilian Batterers by Education

Education	Active Military		Civilians	
	N	%	N	%
Less than high school	46	19.9	144	58.3
High school/GED	149	64.5	80	32.4
More than high school	36	15.6	23	9.3
Total[a]	231	100.0	247	100.0

[a]Totals vary as not all respondents answered this question.

Table 4–3
Frequency Distribution of Military and Civilian Batterers by Ethnicity

Ethnicity	Active Military		Civilians	
	N	%	N	%
Anglo/German	67	28.6	148	57.2
Black	123	52.6	70	27.0
Hispanic	41	19.5	41	15.8
Totals[a]	231	100.0	259	100.0

[a]Totals vary as not all respondents answered this question.

married to black males, five were married to Hispanic males, and one was married to an Oriental. Five abused black women were married to whites and one to an Hispanic. Among the other combinations were nine German women married to whites, blacks, and Hispanics.

Nancy K. Raiha, a captain in the U.S. Army and a social worker, sees such a trend as the product of the melting pot atmosphere inherent in the mobile military lifestyle. Such marriages contain many potential strains. She writes:

> In any intercultural marriage differences in norms, values, expectations, and habits may lead to tension and conflict. Social pressures (i.e., discrimination) are sometimes an additional burden to the interracial couple. The foreign-born may not only have to deal with an alien environment, but also with a language barrier. Couples who are unable to communicate verbally seem more likely in some cases to resort to physical means of expressing displeasure and frustration.[12]

One case may illustrate the constellation of problems, psychological as well as cultural, that can interact in such situations.

> Merta's husband met her while he was stationed in Greece. They were married there, and then he was reassigned to Texas. Merta admittedly had a very naive idea of life in the United States, not to mention what she expected of living in Texas. She spoke little English. Her media-inspired images of this country mainly revolved around unparalleled affluence and violence, particularly gangster and street crime, Mitch, her husband, showed the same sorts of obsessive jealousy and domination that many other researchers have noted in studies of civilian batterers. He played on her Hollywood stereotypes and portrayed life in the United States as one of continuous fear of muggings, rapes, and kidnappings. Mitch forbade Merta ever to leave the house, for whatever reason, without his accompanying her. Stores, post offices, and shopping malls were death traps, he warned her. Gradually he narrowed their outside excursions down to one weekly trip to the supermarket. She was forbidden ever to leave his side or speak to anyone. Ironically, not long before he beat her for something as innocent as speaking to a postal carrier and she escaped to the women's shelter (she had seen its advertisement on television), he had won a Sergeant of the Year award.

The Violence

Our earlier research on violence in civilian families had been an unsettling experience. After cataloging a long, sad list of ways in which men beat women, we extrapolated figures based on the number of women who contacted the Dallas–Fort Worth shelter in a given year and estimated that many tens of thousands of women annually were victims of serious abuse in that single urban region.

We were unprepared, however, for the severity of violence we encountered in the military cases. Table 4–4 compares our military and civilian samples on specific forms of violence. In both groups there was a high incidence of verbal abuse (name-calling, swearing, and so on). Likewise, in both groups the majority of men slapped and punched women. For some types of violence, such as kicking, burning, and sexual abuse, the civilian men tended to stop short of committing acts that would permanently injure, maim, or kill women. Less so was the restraint among the soldiers. For example, more than half the civilian men threatened to use a weapon on the women, compared to half as many soldiers who threatened. But almost twice as many soldiers as civilians actually used weapons on women. Four in ten military batterers used everything from guns and knives to baseball bats, lamps, and belts. A total of sixteen military men shot or pistol-whipped their wives, and twenty-two soldiers injured women with knives.

Much of this violence was gruesome and hardly the result of a man suddenly losing his temper. For example, one soldier took a bayonet and cut off one of his wife's breasts. Another pummeled both his wife and his preadolescent son into unconsciousness with his fists, then forced a long cylindrical object up the anuses of each as they lay sprawled on the kitchen floor, literally ripping out their rectal tissues. (Doctors who later examined the boy and his mother never could determine precisely what the husband had inserted into them.)

There was a good deal of lethal behavior that did not involve weapons. Compared to less than one out of ten civilian men, more than four out of

Table 4–4
Summary of Battering Forms and Frequency of Occurrence among Military and Civilian Batterers

Battering Form	Active Military		Civilians	
	N	%	N	%
Slaps	166	71.5	241	88.9
Kicks	91	39.2	192	70.8
Punches	149	64.2	212	78.2
Burning	13	5.5	35	12.9
Sexual abuse	38	16.4	67	24.7
Threats to use weapons	62	28.9	150	55.4
Use of weapon	91	40.4	60	22.1
Other	69	29.2	66	24.4
Battering while pregnant	67	28.4	122	45.0
Choking	106	44.9	21	7.7
Throwing the victim	157	67.7		
Throwing objects	83	35.8		

ten soldiers choked their wives into unconsciousness or hard enough to leave sore and bruised windpipes and neck muscles. More than two-thirds of the military wives were thrown around rooms (into walls or over furniture). One man flew into a rage over a disagreement at the dinner table, threw a glass of wine into his wife's eyes (the glass *and* the wine), pulled her by the throat across the dining room table and dinner dishes, threw her down one flight of stairs into the basement, and locked her there for the entire night.

Perhaps it is the category of other that contains the most bizarre and pathologically suggestive violence. Both civilians and military men committed other forms of violence that could not be placed in one of the other categories in about one-fourth of the cases, but the military examples were of a much different order of severity. For example, we had known of civilian men who would restrain or even tie women's hands behind their backs with extension cords, chain them to bedposts, and so forth. We saw worse violence in the military cases, such as one man who literally bit his wife up and down each arm—from wrist to shoulder—until his teeth punctured her skin and drew blood. One fellow made it a practice to strangle family pets (mostly cats and dogs) in front of his children to warn them about the consequences of disobeying; once he literally tore off the head of his son's hamster during such a discipline lecture. In other cases the violence took equally pathological, if exotic, forms. One soldier regularly tied his wife to a chair and locked her in a bedroom closet every day before he went on duty and untied her and let her out in the evenings when he returned home. During the day she heard and saw nothing, nor could she eat, drink, relieve herself, or even move.

Granted, these are horror stories, but they are true. Moreover, they were simply the ones we had readily at hand as we began writing. There were many more cases as bad or worse. And that is the point: The worst of the civilian cases were the norm for the military cases.

The Injuries

Injuries suffered by the military wives in our sample matched the severity of the soldiers' violence, as table 4–5 displays. While it is generally true that less serious injuries, such as bruises, cuts, and burns were more frequently reported for civilian women, the more serious injuries tended to occur in military families. For example, more than half of these women had been abused while pregnant, and one-third of them later developed complications in their pregnancies that threatened their own lives as well as those of their unborn children.

Table 4–5
Summary of Injuries and Frequency of Occurrence among Military and Civilian Batterers

Type of Injury	Active Military		Civilians	
	N[a]	%	N[b]	%
Broken glasses or hair pulling	107	46.1	16	6.1
Bruises	179	77.2	251	95.4
Cuts	73	31.3	133	50.6
Burns	6	2.6	63	24.0
Broken Bones	16	6.9	29	11.0
Abuse while pregnant	125	56.6		
Complications with pregnancy	41	23.8	55	20.9
Other	133	57.1	21	8.0

Note: The numbers vary as not all respondents answered this question.
[a]N = 236 (total)
[b]N = 263 (total)

The Life-Endangerment Index

The seriousness of the violence in military families can best be seen through a measure we call the CSR (Center for Social Research) Life Endangerment Index. We divided the forms of abuse cited in the previous section and the type of injuries received into two categories: life-endangering and non-life-endangering. The forms of abuse we considered life-endangering were choking, use of a weapon, and other. Other was included because the violent actions counted in this category—such as smothering, holding the woman's head under water, starvation, or drugging—frequently could have resulted in death. We realize that in some cases non-life-endangering abuse also might have resulted in the death of the woman (for example, verbal abuse could lead to suicide, or sexual abuse could cause internal bleeding and death), but by including only the most obvious forms of abuse in the life-endangering category, we constructed a conservative estimate that could not easily be accused of exaggeration.

Types of injuries received by the women also were divided into life-endangering and non-life-endangering. The categories that we regarded as non-life-endangering were none, broken glasses or pulled hair, and bruises. All other types of injuries posed more direct threats to the women's lives, especially other. (Other here contained diverse injuries such as amputations, internal bleeding and wounds, and comas.)

We then awarded weighted points for the various violent acts and types of injuries considered life-endangering. We combined them into a single measure we term the CSR Life Endangerment Index. Further details on scoring can be found in appendix A. With this measure we then classified each family violence case as one of four types:

Non-life-endangering,

Moderately life-endangering,

Severely life-endangering,

Dangerously life-endangering.

Moreover, we compared the scores of the military families with the scores of the civilian sample to obtain some idea of just how violent the military cases were.

The results are presented in table 4–6 and clearly show that the instances of violence in military families tend in the more lethal direction. In fact, three-fourths of the military cases were in the dangerously life-endangering category compared to only about one-third of the civilian cases.

Thus there is no question that the instances of family violence occurring over a several-year period at or around Fort Hood, Texas, involved much more serious violence than did civilian cases occurring in nonmilitary communities at about the same time. The task remaining is to explain why.

The Military Effect

Ours is the first study to contrast a group of violent male soldiers with violent male civilians. Suffice it to say that we have ventured into unexplored territory. Once salient differences have been discovered, however, it is a much different (and more difficult) matter to account for them. In the course of analyzing these findings, we heard two explanations, or more correctly, speculations, as to why some military men are so violent toward loved ones in their homes. It is worth considering each of these briefly.

Table 4–6
Relationship between Military Experience and Life Endangerment Index

Score	Active Military		Civilians	
	N	%	N	%
Non-life-endangering	0	0.0	4	1.5
Life-endangering	5	2.1	9	3.3
Severely life-endangering	55	23.5	156	56.9
Dangerously life-endangering	174	74.4	105	38.3
Totals	234	100.0	274	100.0

Note: $N = 689$; $X = 74.689$; Probability $= .001$

Violent Personalities Self-Select into the Military

Self-selection is a social process in which persons recruit themselves. They are already predisposed, or conditioned, to be attracted to certain groups or ideas and actively seek these out. According to this logic, the military attracts a certain element of citizens who have authoritarian, violence-prone personalities. The military, after all, is the institution with the supreme capacity for lethal violence and destruction and one that overtly indoctrinates and prepares its members for possible mass-scale fighting. Personalities who are high in frustration, aggressive tendencies, and hostility; exhibit a low self-esteem; and have a host of other possible psychological problems might self-select themselves into a branch of the military service, particularly when the military offers a number of incentives to make recruitment more attractive.

The Army's Captain Nancy K. Raiha warns against assuming that all or most service members have such personality traits, but she describes this theory as follows:

> There may be reason to suspect that more traditional and rigid types would find military life a comfortable existence. Sociologists who postulate that successful fighting units are formed through a process of male-bonding might lead one to believe that a more "macho" male would fit in well in combat units. . . . the tendency of young people to join the service to escape unsatisfactory home situations may increase the number of service men and women who had unstable or violent parental models.[13]

In our conversations with U.S. Army officers (who had professional reasons to defend military training procedures), they attributed spouse abuse to personality defects in the volunteer troops. The end of the draft and the Army's need for men meant a lowering of standards. In short, increasing numbers of "trash" (as one put it) had entered the military. These bad apples were causing such problems.

A fear of such consequences from the volunteer Army was expressed indirectly several years ago in an article by Joseph A. Califano, Jr., former assistant to Secretary of Defense Robert McNamara, once special assistant for domestic affairs to President Lyndon B. Johnson, and former secretary of the Department of Health, Education, and Welfare. He warned that an all-volunteer Army would be class-biased:

> By design and incentive an all-volunteer army is structured to bring into the armed forces the poor and near poor and to free of even the danger of military service the middle class. . . . It legislates into government policy the Civil War practice of having the better off hire the worse-off to serve their time in the military.[14]

Although Califano did not explicitly say as much, he implied elsewhere in that article that the motives to serve of these poorer and lower class mercenaries would be less patriotic and more the by-product of their poverty and personalities.

Certainly the personality argument is tempting, given the horrendous examples of violence and cruelty we found in just a few hundred case files of violent military families. Actual evidence of it is meager, however, Psychologist Peter A. Neidig and several colleagues measured self-esteem, attitudes toward others, (traditional) attitudes of men toward women, the ability to empathize with others, and dogmatic styles of thinking (among other things) in two groups. The first group was made up of forty married active duty service personnel with records of known domestic violence. The second or control group of similar military men had no such records of past violence. On the basis of their findings Neidig and his co-workers rejected the personality hypothesis. They found, instead that the key is a soldier's ability to cope with stress, both on the job and in the marriage. Personality and attitude measures were of little use for understanding violent men.[15]

In addition, we did not find compelling support for the bad apple personality explanation in our military sample. As tables 4–7 and 4–8 show, the sorts of childhood or adolescent experiences that logically ought to affect men's ideas about violence, particularly violence directed at women, are not

Table 4–7
Frequency Distribution of Batterers Witnessing Spouse Abuse between Parents

	Active Military		Civilians	
	N	%	N	%
Yes	106	57.6	136	58.6
No	78	42.4	96	41.4
Totals[a]	184	100.0	232	100.0

[a]Totals vary as not all respondents answered this question.

Table 4–8
Frequency Distribution of Batterers Physically Abused as a Child

	Active Military		Civilians	
	N	%	N	%
Yes	40	24.7	86	37.6
No	122	75.3	143	62.4
Totals	162	100.0	229	100.0

unique to violent military men. Equal proportions of active military men and civilian men reportedly witnessed physical violence between their parents. In fact, the military batterers actually were less likely to have been physically abused as children than were the civilians.

Thus, at this time there does not seem to be much evidence (aside from intuition and hunches) that violent military men are a different psychological breed from nonviolent military men. We will have to look elsewhere, or beyond, the psyches of violent military men for the sources of their violence.

Learning and Accepting Violence: The Military Effect

Strain and stress, as Neidig and his colleagues pointed out, help us in understanding domestic violence by soldiers more than do measures of personality or character attributes. Violence, in other words, is more a response or limited way of coping with a frustrating situation than some programmed trait. It is a style of actions conditioned by past experiences, prejudices, and emotional needs poorly controlled.

The difference between interpreting this violence as a personality trait or as a style of dealing with problems is important. Violent personalities would require profound changes and complex, prolonged therapies to transform them. But if violence is simply a style or technique of handling stress, then alternative techniques can be taught and substituted. We need not psychoanalyze or do depth analysis on every dream and doodle of soldiers. We can intervene by teaching nonviolent techniques to control anger and make for better ways to cope with stress, using education as much or more than therapy.

Strain, as psychologist Neidig and others claim, is undoubtedly part of the problem. But strain by itself is not the complete explanation of the violence. All our cases of family violence involved peacetime soldiers—not soldiers in wartime, not soldiers going through the macho indoctrination of boot camp, not soldiers burdened with the crushing pressure of, say, the responsibility to push a button and launch the missiles of World War III. Rather, their strains were more comparable to those of clerks and junior executives in civilian corporations. In addition, we can assume that such strains were fairly equally distributed among many more soldiers, some of whom undoubtedly also beat their wives but many more of whom did not.

Our own suspicion, based on facts we present below, is that there exists a military effect, a term by which we mean the total impact of the military indoctrination/socialization experience. This includes not just boot camp but also the fighter spirit routinely reinforced by the military's authority pyramid and its creation of stressful situations. The military effect legitimatizes a pervasive sense (and expectation) of violence. For most military men and their families, it is a contained violence, disciplined and therefore merely a potential. For some soldiers, however, the fighter spirit helps amplify traditional sexist attitudes, poor anger control, and even personality or emotional problems. The military effect, in other words, acts itself out pathologically and destructively in cases when a constellation of factors come into play.

A reasonable question to ask is "Does the military effect generalize?" That is, is there a measurable spillover effect into the civilian community close to a base? If so, we would expect that the very proximity of civilians to a large enough installation (large enough in this case meaning that program installation has an important effect on the local economy and other parts of the community) would infuse or contaminate them with some of the military ethos. Likewise, we might predict that persons who had once been exposed to the military effect but are not now in active service (that is, veterans) might show residues of this exposure. Logically they ought to show less severe signs of family violence than active military abusers but more severe signs than violent men who had never served in the military.

To test these possibilities, we drew on all the families analyzed in our earlier study of Dallas–Fort Worth violent families as well as all the families in the shelter adjacent to Fort Hood. Each group of families was divided into three subgroups of families for whom we had complete information: active military personnel, veterans, and civilians who had never served in the military. Then we compared their average scores on the CSR Life Endangerment Index.

The results, as displayed in table 4–9 and figure 4–1, reveal how pervasive and lasting the military effect seems to be. Military families in the military town experienced slightly more severe violence than did veterans' families, and the veterans in turn experienced slightly more severe violence in their families than did the families of civilians who had never been soldiers. The average life endangerment scores of all subgroups in the military town are not terribly different, however.

The same trend occurs in the Dallas–Fort Worth groups. Active military families (though admittedly we are handicapped by having only seven of

Table 4–9
Summary of Mean CSR Life Endangerment Index Score for Sample Types in Killeen and Dallas–Forth Worth, Texas

	Active Military		Veterans		Civilians		Total	
	N	$\bar{X}$	N	$\bar{X}$	N	$\bar{X}$	N	$\bar{X}$
Killeen	234	3.722	32	3.688	61	3.672	333	3.684
Dallas–Fort Worth	7	3.429	181	3.359	274	3.321	526	3.260

Note: Killeen is a military town.
Ns vary as not all respondents answered this question.

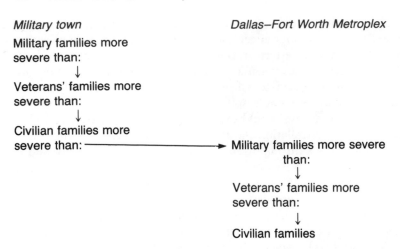

Figure 4–1. Ranked Severity of Violence in Two Communities

them) experienced slightly more severe violence than veterans' families who saw slightly more severe violence than civilians' families.

The true extent of the military effect becomes clearer when we compare the subgroups in the different locations. For instance, the military families in the military town had higher average life endangerment scores than military families in Dallas–Fort Worth. The same is true for veterans: Those near the military installation were more severely violent than those in Dallas–Fort Worth. Even civilians in Dallas–Fort Worth were less violent than civilians in the military town. And the most telling support for the military effect is that civilians in the military town had higher average life endangerment scores than the military persons in Dallas–Fort Worth.

In sum, families in the Texas military-dominated community—whether active military, veteran, or civilian—on the average experienced more severe violence than veterans, and veterans tended to be more violent than civilians. The most important factor, however, was not so much one's military or nonmilitary status but whether one lived in a military-dominated town. Those living in a military-dominated community tended to be more violent than those living in a nonmilitary community.

The military effect is one type of more general phenomenon known to social scientists. They term it a contextual effect—that is, the ethos and cultural climate of a community can make many actions and attitudes more likely than they would be in some other climate. For example, Travis Hirschi and Rodney Stark wrote an article titled "Hellfire and Delinquency" that tested the common sense idea that teenagers who go to church more often will be less prone to become juvenile delinquents. They found otherwise.

Church attendance and religion seemed to make no difference in keeping youth on the straight and narrow, and for years this finding was generally accepted as fact.[16]

Some years later Stark returned to the issue. By this time other researchers had studied general church attendance in the communities in which Stark and Hirschi and others had done the original studies on individual delinquents and religion. Stark found in reanalyzing both types of data that religion and church attendance did make a difference, but contextually. As Stark explains it:

> It is not whether an individual kid goes to church or believes in hell that influences his or her delinquency. What is critical is whether the *majority* of the kid's *friends* are religious. In communities where most young people do not attend church, religion will not inhibit the behavior even of those teenagers who personally are religious. However, in communities where most kids are religious, then those who are will be less delinquent than those who aren't.[17]

In other words, the religious effect on delinquency, could show up only in a community where religious behavior was frequent enough, not in one where church attendance was low. To put it another way, the social context of individual behavior encourages and facilitates some types of behavior and influences more than others.

Now consider the military effect, for it operates in the same way. In a community where the military establishment's presence looms large, not only active military personnel but veterans and even civilians who never served in the military beat women more severely than their counterparts in communities where the military presence is not so marked. The military effect of a huge installation is so pronounced in a modest-sized community that its violent civilian citizens abuse women more severely than do soldiers in a much larger community where the military presence is less visible. The final, unresolved issue, therefore, seems to be one of context and relative size: How important is the active military presence to a community's ethos, economy, and population?

A Final Word

We have stated our findings clearly and in a way that other investigators with larger samples from more diverse settings can attempt to replicate. These findings do, of course, raise many questions that we cannot answer. For example, would military personnel in more technical assignments (as opposed to cavalry and infantry), such as in missile silos, submarines, or Air

Force hangers, manifest this military effect? How large does the military presence have to be in a community—or what is the critical ratio of military installation size to community size—before the military effect spills over into nonactive or nonmilitary families? Do veterans in our study show residues of the military effect simply because of their past military experiences or because they were reservists who still reassumed the active military role for temporary periods? (We could not tell who was in the active reserve and who was not.)

5
Religion and Family Violence

The hardest men to counsel are the older, religious men. They are stubborn, and they never stop referring to the Bible.
—John Patrick, counselor, Family
Preservation Project of Tyler, Texas

Religion is as old an institution as the family. No anthropologist or archaeologist has ever found any evidence of a society or even a tribe that we could call human that did not show signs of having a religion. These two institutions are still inextricably intertwined in American society. Except for odd cults that cater to idealistic young, single, college-aged students, the fundamental membership unit of churches is still the family, not the individual.

More than a decade has passed since family violence has become recognized as a serious societal problem. Therefore, we might expect that the question of how religion relates to this problem already would have been examined. But in fact the relation of religion to family violence has been virtually ignored. The only exceptions in this research vacuum are studies dealing with exotic religions. For instance, J. Gordon Melton, an ordained minister, a renowned scholar of American religions, and the director of the Institute for the Study of American Religion, found that child abuse and other forms of family violence in controversial new religions (such as the "Moonies" of the Unification Church and the Hare Krishnas) were not remarkably high. Melton concluded that it probably was equal to the amount occurring in conventional churches and denominations.[1] Sociologist Janet Jacobs looked at sexual exploitation, rape, and woman abuse in several cult and sect groups, interviewing ex-members as to how religious beliefs were used to rationalize these practices. She found that religion, in some cases, offered men ready justification for sexist domination and battering.[2]

Overall, however, religion's link to family violence has remained pretty much untouched by researchers. Writers on child abuse sometimes allude to biblical prescriptions about sparing the rod and spoiling the child. Yet until now how religion might actually affect family violence—particularly spouse abuse—for better or worse and how churches might deal with the problem among their members generally have been ignored.

In this chapter we begin a serious look at how religion relates to family violence. We say begin because the broad variety of American religious groups requires a much more extensive study before we can make specific statements about which churches and denominations have more family violence than others. Specifically we want to analyze how religious beliefs and practices (such as relying on the Bible and talking with ministers) affected the lives of couples who experienced family violence. We ask questions such as the following: Did religion contribute to the violence by indirectly helping violent men excuse it (that is, by defining the man as head, disciplinarian, or otherwise of the household)? Or did religion mute or discourage the violence by providing reference to nonviolent messages in scriptures? Furthermore, how did persons and victims see their own violence in terms of their religious beliefs?

Our goal is not to disparage any religious groups. Rather, we want to make a frank assessment of any connection between religious beliefs and activities and spouse abuse. Eventually we hope to be able to suggest ways in which religious groups (as an important resource in any community) can more constructively confront the mounting family violence problem.

The Double-Edged Sword

Religion can be all things to all people. To those who want to uphold and justify the status quo, religion can be used to calm discontent, apologize for injustices, and divert energies away from social change. (This is why Karl Marx, the father of communism, once referred to religion as the "opiate of the masses."[3]) Other religious values can be used as a reason for working to create change, as Americans witnessed during the late 1950s and 1960s in the form of the civil rights movement.

Religion has such possible connections to family violence, being a double-edged sword that can as easily rationalize violence, particularly against women, as condemn it. There are two opposite scenarios in which religion defines women's roles and that would determine how religion is linked to abuse. The first is a conservative, traditionalist version and the second a change-oriented, liberating version.

Scenario 1: Religion as a Conservative Force

Both Judaism and Christianity (as well as Islam) arose in cultures that were patriarchal. Men controlled the wealth and wrote the laws. Physical strength was a valued attribute for everyday affairs, prized not just for labor but also for fighting. Birth control was nonexistent (except for those choosing abstinence), and most occupations could be placed in one of two categories: male or female. In this scenario the influence of these patriarchal cultures on the men who wrote the various books of the Bible makes Judaic-Christian religion a force not just for restricting women in how they may act but also for justifying (however subtly) punishment of unruly women or women who failed to honor their husbands.

One does not have to be a biblical scholar to find instances of this male-dominated worldview throughout the Bible. For example, in the New Testament, Saint Paul, who helped spread Christianity throughout the non-Jewish world of the first century Roman Empire, wrote in a letter to his protégé Timothy about women's proper demeanor in church:

> Women should be dressed neatly, their adornment being modesty and serious-mindedness. It is not for them to have an elaborate hairstyle, jewelry of gold or pearls, or expensive clothes, but, as becomes women who profess to believe in God, it is for them, to show their faith by the way they live. A women should learn quietly and humbly. Personally, I don't allow women to teach, nor do I ever put them in authority over men—I believe they should be quiet.[4]

Saint Paul reasoned that women's subordinate place in ancient society was justified because, according to the Old Testament, Adam had been created before Eve and that it was Eve, not Adam, who was first deceived by Satan in the Garden of Eden and who first fell into sin. Saint Paul even believed that women would have safer, less arduous deliveries during childbirth if they maintained lives of "faith, love, holiness, and modesty." Modesty for Saint Paul meant that women accepted a submissive, inferior role to men. Likewise, in one letter he gave the Christians at the struggling church in Corinth explicit guidelines for directing women's subservient behavior:

> Let women be silent in church; they are not to be allowed to speak. They must submit to this regulation, as the [Jewish] law itself instructs. If they have questions to ask they must ask their husbands at home, for there is something improper about a woman's speaking in church.[5]

Paul even recommended against marriage, since marriage (that is, the woman's concerns) took up too much of a man's time. Paul did concede that if a man's physical needs were so powerful that he "burned" and was preoccupied with women, then the man should marry. Otherwise, Paul advised, men would do better to remain celibate like himself.

What we have done, of course, is to engage in what theologians call proof-texting, taking some verse or portion of the Bible and using it to prove the immediate point we want to make. Religious sexists can find support for their sexual discrimination in such verses. A large number of Christians, including many conservatives, proof-text when they want to rationalize their behavior, and there is no reason that a violent Christian man could not do the same.

Erling Jorstad, a historian, has written about what he calls the submission school of thinking currently popular with many evangelical Christians. Marabelle Morgan, for instance, preaches that sexual intimacy is a joy and God-given blessing for a Christian couple. She is in favor of women taking a more aggressive attitude in keeping romance alive in marriages. In her "Total Woman" seminars she advocates that women, especially homemaking wives, should eagerly await their husbands when they arrive home after work in erotic negligées and prepare intimate candlelight dinners.

Jorstad, however, says that there is a hidden sexist agenda behind such advice:

> Her [Morgan's] recommendations result directly from her concept of the wife being in submission to her husband, to adopt to his interest, to be what he wants her to be. Morgan writes that this is part of God's plan and the wife's responsibility to God and to her husband.[6]

One survey of five hundred Texas residents similarly found that persons who rated high in traditional religious orthodoxy and those who belonged to conservative religious denominations not only held more traditional sex role attitudes than nonreligious persons, but that the former also were much less likely to believe forced intercourse between a man and his wife was undesirable.[7]

The basic point is that the physical differences between men and women supposedly determine that women have a God-ordained nature to be men's obedient helpers. Other outspoken conservatives, such as Phyllis Schlafly, have argued the same message. In April 1985 the wives of Reverend Jimmy Draper, pastor of the First Baptist Church of Euless, Texas, and a well-known Southern Baptist leader, and Russell Dilday, president of that denomination's Southwestern Theological Seminary, shared the speaker's platform at a day-long conference on Christian living held in Fort Worth. Carol Ann Draper said that her main responsibility was to God, then "to be the wife (my husband) needs me to be." She proclaimed that obedience had been important to her all her life. Mrs. Draper's speech to Southern Baptist women was titled "Accepting Your Circumstances."[8]

It is possible that some violent men could rationalize spouse abuse by claiming some patriarchal authority. More importantly, however, violence could be part of an overall worldview in which a woman's primary responsibility in her marriage, religiously speaking, is to be submissive to her husband. And if she fell down in meeting that key domestic responsibility—or if her husband claimed she did—then there would be grounds for a beating.

Scenario 2: Religion as a Revolutionary Force

Liberals who want religion to justify some social change can proof-text from the Bible just as well as conservatives who resist change. For example, Saint Paul can be interpreted as refuting sexism, as when he wrote to the First Century Christians in Galatia: "All of you who were baptized 'into' Christ have put on the family likeness of Christ. Gone is the distinction between Jew and Greek, slave and freeman, male and female—you are all one in Christ Jesus."[9]

Thus in this second possible scenario religious values could erode rationalizations of patriarchal authority and sexism instead of emphasizing the inequality and misery involved in spouse abuse. Certainly there is ample evidence that religion and religious values have been associated with helping liberate women from traditional, restrictive roles. Religious institutions, both Protestant and Catholic, currently are witnessing an explosion of movements to ordain women as clergy and include them in the highest administrative offices. In face, many innovators in the history of American religion, white and black, have been women. Among these are Ellen White, Mary Baker Eddy, and Anna Maria Smith. Typical of these was Anna Howard Shaw, the first woman ordained in the Methodist Protestant Church in 1880. In later years she became president of the National Woman's Suffrage Association.[10]

One national survey, despite contradictory findings, even suggested that men and women without any religious affiliation had the highest rates of spousal violence, particularly when it was the man abusing the woman. The reasons were far from clear, however.[11]

Consequently, there is no logical reason that we should not expect to find religion's relation to family violence to be a positive, constructive one working against violence. This could take forms such as ministers advising battered women to go to shelters and batterers to seek special counseling or finding that regular churchgoers actually are less likely to be violent in the home than nonchurchgoers.

Whether religion reinforces or discourages family violence is, of course, something we can examine directly. In the remainder of this chapter we turn to actual evidence of how religion was involved in marriage and romantic relationships where spouse abuse occurred.

Religion in the Lives of Violent Couples

Many social scientists have conducted studies that asked Americans about their religious beliefs and practices. A growing number is asking other Americans about their own experiences of violence. Unfortunately, few scientists ask the same people about both their religious lives and their exposure to family violence. We were fortunate, therefore, to work with one colleague who attempted to tap both worlds by asking university students about the occurrence of courtship and dating violence they had encountered as well as their religious backgrounds and habits.[12] The topic needs much more research, but the first results of the study were intriguing.

Most of the young adults in our colleague's study were single and therefore less active in churches and organized religion. If they were violent in their romantic relationships or experienced violence, we can assume that they were probably only just beginning to commit milder forms of abuse. Therefore, the study did not find large, dramatic differences among the adherents of various denominations and sects. Yet we did see one suggestive pattern. When Protestants were grouped into clusters we called conservatives (Church of Christ, all Lutherans, Southern as well as Independent Baptists, Pentecostals, Nazarenes, Seventh Day Adventists, and Mormons) and moderates (United Methodists, Presbyterians, and Episcopalians), conservatives were abusive 49 percent of the time compared to moderates 45 percent of the time. Admittedly those figures are extremely close. But when we rated each case's abuse as mildly, moderately, or seriously (life-threatening) abusive, we found that no moderate respondent was in the seriously abusive category compared to 6 percent of the conservatives. This is not an earth-shaking statistic to be sure, but it did make us wonder what a more sensitive, focused questionnnaire given to a more representative sample of citizens might disclose.

We discovered one other intriguing statistic in our attempt to understand the relationship between religion and spouse abuse. In chapter 2 we presented a Psychological Self-Inventory of questions, presented in table 2–7, that violent men in counseling had answered about themselves. We asked one additional question with religious overtones: "How much were you bothered by feeling you should be punished for your sins?" Half the abusive men answered that they had been bothered by this feeling.

We also had other information. To unravel the dynamics of religion's effects on violence, we drew on interviews with the counselors of the Austin Family Violence Diversion Network and the Tyler Family Preservation Project (both described in chapter 2) as well as the case files of clients in these programs. While we had information on religious attitudes and practices for only a portion of the men passing through the Austin program, such information was available for most of the Tyler program participants. Overall, one-third of the sixty-three Tyler clients spoke about religion and its relation to their violence, even though neither program utilized religious appeals or themes in counseling or even brought up the subject unless clients wished to discuss it. These persons spoke of their strict religious upbringings, often apologetically, as if they considered themselves backsliders. Although most men and women in counseling made no mention of church activity or religious involvement in their earlier lives, it is still worth considering the group that did speak of religion. How religion became an important element in their violence may point to yet another handle on understanding and eventually correcting the problem.

How Religion Was Used to Justify Violence

With few exceptions the several dozen men who spontaneously mentioned religion during counseling did so in defending their use of violence. As scenario 1 would predict, they appealed to the Bible and to their natural patriarchal rights as heads of their households. The most common word they used was *submit*: She will not submit, she did not submit, she should submit. The women's lack of obedience to men, in other words, was in their opinion the real root of the problem. One typical religious client, Jerry, wanted his wife to submit to him because the Bible said she should. Her rebellious nature caused him to have to discipline her, he claimed.

Other men used a more subtle rationalization: The woman's submission to her husband was really her way of submitting to God, thus her disobedience was not simply a problem she had with her husband's authority. She was not following God's will. Several men who had received advice from fundamentalist Christian counselors offered such a logic to excuse their anger and beatings. For example, Max was convinced that much of his family's violence problem would disappear if he only could convince his wife to join in family prayer and discussion sessions. His children resisted and resented even more being forced to attend fundamentalist church services on Saturdays. His religious demands increased the tension within his family and did as much to promote violence as to reduce it.

Several men even brought God's immediate, personal approval of their wife-beating into the picture. Sydney, an overbearing husband, believed that he received direct revelations from God. Therefore, he claimed he knew clearly what God wanted. God told him that if his wife, Edie, would just become "more righteous" and submit to Sydney's orders, their relationship's problems would "straighten right out." Another man, Mark, was eventually diagnosed as a schizophrenic and institutionalized (after forcing his wife to play Russian roulette with a loaded revolver). Mark's wife, a zealous fundamentalist, constantly cited her minister as the ultimate authority on all family matters. Mark began claiming that God spoke regularly to him and not to the minister as a way of reducing the minister's influence over his wife.

Such extreme cases aside, the most ominous use of religion occurred when men freely admitted that they had been violent but that since they had been "saved" by Jesus Christ, all their sins and weaknesses, including explosive anger, were forgiven. Worse than instances where men tried to appeal to some bibically defined right to discipline women, these men simply wrote off their violence as an unimportant foible. Their faith, they said, excused them entirely.

Sociologist Janet Jacobs studied a number of battered women who had left charismatic Christian movements and more exotic cult groups and found the same pattern. One woman, Joan, represented the most common case. Joan had gone to her (male) pastor about her husband's violence. Reports Jacobs: "He told her that if she created a good Christian home and was an obedient wife, her husband would have no reason to be abusive." Such a woman's abuse, in other words, was to be explained by her failure to be compliant before her husband, not in the husband's assaults, which the minister dismissed as symptoms of the underlying problem of her rebellious nature. Jacobs summed up this type of abuse:

> Joan's case was similar to that of the other accounts reported by women who had been part of small charismatic church groups. Each of the followers had been beaten by their husbands and had been told that the fault was clearly theirs. They had failed to provide a good Christian home and to serve their husband's needs.[13]

This pattern of men using religious justifications for beatings was matched by many women who believed in the submissive ideal themselves. Most of the violent men who argued that their violence was biblically acceptable and only discipline intended to make things run more smoothly in the family also had wives who struggled to reconcile similar beliefs with the pain of battering. Frequently this passive behavior won them temporary reprieves from beatings, giving them hope (reinforced by what ministers told them) that a more servile role would end the violence. For instance, Julie felt that her husband Tim's violence and temper had begun to mellow since they had returned to attending church each week and both had developed "a personal relationship with Jesus." She claimed Jesus had shown her that Tim was to be the head of the household and that she was to be more submissive to him. In the end, however, she discovered, as did virtually all these women, that the violence persisted and that they were at times in serious physical danger.

Another woman, Judy, displayed the ambivalence caused by holding such religious beliefs and yet being assaulted. Even though she came to the Tyler women's shelter, she still maintained that a woman's duty was to submit to her husband "because that's the way it's supposed to be." She even had fundamentalist profamily religious literature forwarded to the shelter while she was a resident there.

Some women clearly adopted fatalistic views of the violence, which they were able to reconcile with their religious faith. In the case of Dennis and Kaye, for example, Kaye said that her religion was the most important thing to her and that her relationship with God would make her strong enough to endure whatever Dennis might do to her. Betty, the wife of a man described several paragraphs earlier, was even more confident when she described her faith as something that would "protect" her. God, she said, would not let serious harm come to her in her marriage.

Sociologist Janet Jacobs found similar rationalizations in her study of religious battered women:

> [A]s the abuse continued, God's love became more and more important, the emphasis on their spiritual life reflecting the pain and rejection experienced in the material world. Because access to the spiritual realm remained within the control of the male hierarchy, the devotee's sense of powerlessness was often overwhelming. Thus she stayed tied to the church and the domestic relationship that the church sanctioned until the abuse became intolerable and/or life-threatening.[14]

Jacobs reports that such women also are psychologically abused in the sense that they are accused of being worthless, wicked, and unchristian if they disagree with men's submission demands. If they try to find consolation from female friends, they are accused of harboring a "spirit of homosexuality." Seeking help from male friends, not unexpectedly, brings accusations of adultery and a "spirit of lust." For these women religion only prolongs the violence and danger, creating a truly exploitive predicament.

The tragedy in all these cases is that these were women who often naively went to clergymen for help and instead found themselves condemned as immoral. The churches in question actually reinforced the violence, legitimatizing the batterers' behavior and causing a good deal of guilt, depression, and confusion before secular counseling finally was sought.

How Religion Was Used as a Possible Solution to Violence

Before they entered counseling, some men held out hope that religion per se would somehow solve their problem of violence. Those who believed that the real problem lay in their wives' disobedience thought that church attendance would correct the women. It was not unusual for a man suddenly to phone his counselor and announce that he no longer needed therapy (not infrequently on the advice of a minister or fellow church member). One man insisted he did not need to return because his wife had just "found God and made things right with him." He now knew "things would be under control."

Other men admitted that they had a violence problem but once had held similar hopes that religion would miraculously give them some new control over their hostility or resolve issues of tension. Since these men all had eventually come to secular counselors, they were obviously disappointed in the fruits of the religious cure.

Sometimes the men tried religion as a panacea, but it backfired on them. One outstanding example was Fred, whose wife finally convinced him to attend a fundamentalist church on a weekly basis. Fred initially dropped out of the Austin Family Violence Diversion program, convinced that religion (and not secular counseling) was his solution. The problem was that the pastor declared that members should sanctify themselves before coming to the Lord's altar by abstaining from sexual intercourse for twenty-four hours before each church service. Unfortunately, the church held services a minimum of four times each week. Fred eventually became tense over his impoverished sex life and subsequently lapsed into violence once more, returning to the program more frustrated than before.

In one unusual case, Tom found the Lord in a fundamentalist group but deliberately used his faith to increase the tension between him and his wife Gail. He used religion as an excuse to discontinue sexual relations with Gail and refused to divorce her. In the counselor's opinion Tom seemed unconsciously to be driving her to commit adultery (which she eventually did out of frustration) in order to justify battering her. One night Tom broke into her lover's house while she was visiting there. The boyfriend tragically shot and killed Tom in self-defense, then out of guilt committed suicide soon after.

In a relatively few instances religion did serve a positive, healing function. One abusive man had been an abused child, had seen combat as a Marine in Vietnam, and then had served a prison sentence for several years. He admitted at the beginning of counseling that he was seeking some way out of his "bad karma." For a while he had experimented with LSD and trained vigorously in karate. He was an intense person, and he later met an attractive Pentecostal woman and "went at the religion gung ho" (in the words of his counselor). He dropped drugs and martial arts out of his life when he returned to Austin. His church attendance eventually began to slack off, however, and he became abusive toward his wife. In the Austin diversion program a conselor recognized the important role religion had once played in the man's life and recommended that he return to church. He did. He began praying thirty minutes at the church every morning, gave his testimony as a Christian to the diversion program's group of violent men during counseling sessions, and received a good deal of sympathy and group support from them.

The same thing happened to Ron not long after he entered the Austin program. He encountered a Jehovah's Witness missionary and began meeting daily for fellowship and Bible study. He did not abandon secular counseling but instead used his new faith to strengthen his self-esteem and supplement anger-control counseling.

Another positive example was Carl, a man who resented his wife's spending so much time at church and used that as an excuse to batter her. After entering the Austin diversion program, he began reevaluating his and his wife's responsibilities in their marriage as well as learning how to manage his anger. He also began accompanying her to church. In this case their religious experiences brought the couple closer together: He became a serious student in Bible classes and eventually a lay preacher in the church. Other church members were aware of his violence problem and gave him much needed support throughout his counseling. The most significant aspect of Carl's case was that his church was a fundamentalist one, demonstrating that there is nothing inevitable about any version of Christianity that reinforces family violence.

A common pattern found in most of the couples where religion was an element in the violence was the woman's belief that religion would help ameliorate the husband's anger and battering. Many felt that if he would just start going to church, things immediately would begin to improve. As we have shown, sometimes this happened, but more often than not, this idea backfired. The men picked up on the scenario 1 aspects of Christianity and proof-texted segments out of the Bible to justify their violence. Tragically, they sometimes were encouraged to do this by ministers.

Certainly, when a woman bought into the submission theme and the husband's violence did subsequently decrease for a while, the woman felt that religion had helped. At least she could rationalize that the trade-off was an improvement in her physical safety. Yet sometimes the woman's insistence that the man become involved in religion only increased the tension and hostility. Donna was a Jehovah's Witness whose faith was very important to her. Her husband Sam, on the other hand, was uninterested in religion and found her sectarian zeal an irritant (she tirelessly worked at converting him). As a devout Jehovah's Witness, she spent many hours each week witnessing door to door in neighborhoods. Sam held two jobs and simply did not want what free time he had taken up with her religion. They clashed periodically and violently. A vicious circle developed, each beating leaving her more frantic to convert him, and each conversion attempt angering him more.

The Religious Effect in Retrospect

The overwhelming role played by religion in the lives of the violent couples we studied was a regressive, unwholesome one. Religion typically provided violent men with a rationale to dominate women and excused their occasional violence as necessary discipline. In several cases it even intensified the violence. Moreover, the counselors in these two programs believed that even in cases where religion was not explicitly mentioned by male clients, the general values of scenario 1 seemed to run like a red letter throughout the men's rhetoric and rationalizations.

But as we have seen, religion does not necessarily have to be used in this way. It may be that a much larger number of couples would show more examples along the lines of scenario 2. And, of course, we had no way to learn about those couples who received constructive advice from ministers or priests and thus never entered either of the two programs we studied. At the time we wrote this, one of us happened to speak with a Methodist minister who had been the pastor of a small church in Belton, Texas, not far from Fort Hood (the military base discussed in chapter 4). He had dealt personally with families experiencing the type of violence we have analyzed and told of his counseling experiences. We learned that a scenario 2 perspective could work. Anecdotes such as that give us hope that clergy are becoming more sensitive to this violence problem.

Nevertheless, it appears that religion is an important element that must be taken into consideration for a significant proportion of violent families. Spouse abuse also is a problem that more churches and denominations must recognize explicitly. Some already do. The United Methodist denomination, for example, yearly publishes its social principles, or resolutions, concerning various social issues ranging from abortion and homosexuality to medical experimentation. Its 1984 *Book of Resolutions* directly condemned child abuse an spousal violence. The denomination's 1980 publication by its Family Life Committee, titled *Family Life: A Resolution,* states:

> Violence among family members is an issue of special concern. The home should be a place of honest communication where conflict is dealt with construcively. All family members are entitled to physical safety, security, and emotional well-being.[15]

Another example is the Church of Jesus Christ of Latter-day Saints (the Mormons). In the early 1980s Mormon men who applied for a "temple recommends" from their local bishop in order to participate in temple rituals began being queried about any possibly abusive incidents involving wives or chidren. In 1986, at a session of the 156th LDS General Conference in Salt Lake City, Utah, one of us who attended as an observer heard Gordon B. Hinckley, first counselor to LDS president Ezra Taft Benson, bluntly admonish Mormons that spousal violence and child abuse were unequivocally grounds for excommunication if they did not confess and pray for forgiveness.

Alternatively, groups such as the Church of Christ denomination make no formal pronouncements on social issues. This does not mean that conservative Christian groups have to be or are silent on this problem. In one community with which we are familiar, for example, the conservative First (Southern) Baptist Church of Arlington, Texas, started the first women's shelter in that city. Congregation members sat on the shelter's first board of directors, and the church donated the original shelter building and underwrote operating expenses until the shelter could obtain more broad-based funding from United Way and other agencies.

Yet as anyone who follows the newspaper headlines can testify, conservative and evangelical Christianity—precisely the kinds with which our subsample of abusive men most identified—is gaining momentum in our society. Not only are the more biblically orthodox denominations growing while liberal and moderate mainline groups are declining in numbers,[16] but these orthodox groups (in particular the Southern and Independent Baptists and the Pentecostals) are mobilizing to put political muscle behind their traditional views of what constitute appropriate family styles (that is, patriarchal homes in which women are submissive homemakers).[17] They are antiabortion, anti-Equal Rights Amendments, antifeminist, and often opposed to shelters for battered women.

In 1979 ministers and other religious leaders sympathetic to right-wing politics and conservative Christianity organized a Washington for Jesus rally, drawing hundreds of thousands of like-minded citizens to lobby in the nation's capital. That same year Reverend Jerry Falwell created the Moral Majority, Inc., while in California a West Coast version called Christian Voice, Inc., became active about the same time. In 1986 a televangelist named Pat Robertson, founder of the Christian Broadcasting Network and host of *The 700 Club* television program, began openly attending Republican rallies and caucuses, offering himself as a possible presidential candidate. These are but a few of the persons and groups who likely would undo much of what the antiviolence movement has accomplished. The greatest challenge to the religious institution during the remainder of this century vis-à-vis the family will be whether it will use religion's potential to liberate women from inequality and abuse or heed the persistent penchant of some sectarians to turn back the clock on the progressive movement for women's rights, including the basic right of a woman to be physically safe in her own home.

This look at religion's influence on family violence has been limited and extremely exploratory. It is standard practice to call politely for further research at the conclusion of every study. In this instance we have barely scratched the surface of the dynamics of the violence problem and sincerely urge other to consider the effect of religion in their own future studies or their own violent circumstances. Religion is simply too important an institution to ignore any longer.

III
Agenda for Dealing with Violence

While there is now public and official recognition of family violence as a national problem and pressures to confront it, precious little in the way of evaluating existing counseling programs has been done. Since, as we argued in chapter 1, the future of antiviolence programs involves treating perpetrators as well as victims, the time has come to begin identifying effective and noneffective intervention strategies.

In chapter 6 we look at the micro level by evaluating three programs that counsel violent men for anger problems. A number of notions taken from conventional wisdom are tested against the actual results of a follow-up study of once-violent men after counseling. We conclude by outlining what appear to be the more salient characteristics of effective counseling.

In chapter 7 we shift the emphasis to the macro level by setting an agenda for all citizens, both public officials and private individuals. The practical implications of the past six chapters are stressed for those interested in further research as well as those committed to social action. Mobilizing resources and cooperation of any community's many interest groups will not be easy, but only a coordinated strategy offers realistic hope of containing the growing family violence problem.

6
Breaking the Cycle of Family Violence

> Man, I ain't never gonna beat up on a woman again. Nothing will ever make me go through this shit twice!
> —Client overheard during an early meeting of a court-ordered batterers' anger-control program.

W e knew the man who said that. Like most of the men in counseling, he was not always comfortable being there. But eventually he had to confront his violent tendencies and accept responsibility for them. What became of men like him after they graduated from a counseling program?

Money has been tight in the fiscally conservative 1980s. Yet despite large amounts of private and public funds being poured into programs aimed at reducing family violence, accountability for those funds has been virtually nil. Hardly anybody has taken the trouble to see whether they are effective. In one recent survey of almost two hundred treatment programs for violent men in the United States and Canada, the researchers found that none had conducted any follow-up studies on men entering or completing counseling.[1] The truth is that nobody has really been able to say whether programs counseling violent men (and women) succeed in making them nonviolent, or for how long.

The reasons are obvious. Such programs usually are understaffed, underfunded, and overburdened with clients. Most professionals who operate them are counselors, not researchers; their perspectives are clinical, not statistical. And most professionals are not eager to be evaluated by outsiders and possibly open themselves up to criticism.

As a result it is not surprising that there has been a lag between what is being done in these programs and an evaluation of whether they accomplish their goals. This lag has become a political issue in the struggle for limited dollars to fund family violence programs. Woman's shelter advocates understandably are reluctant to support programs for abusive men when such programs not only compete with women's services for a slice of a very modest funding pie but also are still experimental. Feminists criticize untested men's programs for siphoning off funds that are used only to address the most immediate, visible symptom (male violence) of a more deeply based problem in American society—sexism. Without attacking sexism, they claim, the violence potential is never meaningfully removed.

This chapter examines the effectiveness of violence counseling programs for the men whom we studied. We present the results of our own intensive efforts to track down and interview violent men and their spouses after each or both had gone through one of the three counseling agencies described in chapter 2. We wanted to learn answers to the same questions that the average citizen might ask: Do these programs work? Is the violence reduced or eliminated by the counseling, and if so, for how long? What became of men's and women's lives after they or their mates left counseling? How do they now feel about the counseling experience? Would they recommend it to others?

These are practical questions, and it is worthwhile devoting attention to them as soon as possible for two reasons. First, if counseling programs such as the three we put to the test here are not achieving successful results for the time and effort invested in them, then they should be terminated. It would then be time to stop wasting our money, reevaluate our basic assumptions, and look for alternative ways to tackle the male violence problem. Second, if they do work reasonably well, then we should find that out so that we can fine-tune our techniques, make improvements where there are rough spots, and begin using them as basic models for other programs across the country.

The time has come for evaluating all family violence agencies and services that deal with violence problems. Hard-pressed taxpayers who increasingly are expected to foot the bills for such operations deserve no less. In that spirit our own follow-up study of known violent men, one of the first of its kind anywhere, was undertaken to discover whether counseling could break the cycle of male violence.

We also wanted to put certain commonly held assumptions about family violence to the test. In the rush to analyze and draw conclusions about domestic violence, clinicians, counselors, and researchers sometimes have been guilty of constructing a folklore around the subject. For example, during the 1970s one early study by sociologist Richard Gelles, after finding twelve battered women who had witnessed their own parents' violence (eight of whom also were the victims of spouse abuse), asserted that little girls learn to model a victim role from watching their abused mothers.[2] This finding was picked up by other researchers and for years uncritically repeated as fact in the family violence literature. Only in the 1980s have sociologist Mildred Daley Pagelow and others tested the assumption with larger samples to show that this passive generational transfer effect does not hold for females but only for males who learned violence as a technique for dealing with women after watching their fathers.[3] This is an example of what Gelles himself later called the woozle effect—that is, when statements are repeated so often that everyone takes their truth for granted.[4]

Another false assumption in the modern folklore of domestic violence is the revolving door claim that calling the police after such violence and pressing assault charges against abusive men often will not help women, since the men simply will be released on bail and return home twice as angry and even more violent. Lawrence W. Sherman and Richard A. Berk put this bit of folk wisdom to the test over a period of months when they studied violent men who had been arrested because their wives or girfriends pressed assault charges against them. These researchers found the revolving door assumption seriously wanting: Having men arrested by police for domestic assault had a markedly deterrent effect, discouraging many of them from future violence.[5]

Other examples we have heard professionals working in the domestic violence field tout as facts (despite absolutely no evidence to support them) include the idea that programs counseling violent men initially increase male violence against women due to the alleged stress of entering therapy. Another truism commonly repeated is that court-ordered diversion programs (such as in Austin, Texas) can do little for families experiencing violence either because of the revolving door assumption described above or because violent men undergo counseling simply as a ruse to escape criminal convictions.

These beliefs are subjected to actual research, not speculation, in the remainder of this chapter.

The 1984 Follow-up Study in Texas

During the summer of 1984 the authors contracted with the Texas Department of Human Resources to evaluate the effectiveness of three programs counseling violent people.[6] These were the Austin Family Violence Diversion Network, the Family Preservation Program in Tyler, and the Anger Control Program in Arlington, all described in chapter 2.

Using graduate students, counselors, and social workers familiar with the family violence problem, we attempted to locate and interview every person who had entered one of the three programs because of a violence problem. We also made it a point to interview his or her spouse independently. One reason is obvious: A man who was still physically abusing his wife might not tell male interviewers the truth. The woman, interviewed by women, could serve as independent verification of the man's version of life after counseling (we assumed that when these versions differed, the women gave more accurate accounts of what happened than the men). Female interviewers worked from lists of the women, while male interviewers were responsible for the men. The clients were not told that their spouses would be (or had been) contacted.

Interviews were targeted not only at the graduates of these programs but also at terminated clients—that is, those persons who dropped out or were not allowed to continue counseling. (There were various reasons for termination. For example, each program had attendance requirements, and clients could miss only a few sessions with valid excuses before they were dropped. Some clients had drug or alcohol problems that they tried unsuccessfully to hide or would not treat. One enterprising fellow in the Austin program was even caught in the parking lot stealing the hubcaps off other clients' cars during a group session.)

Interviews were conducted with past clients both face to face and by telephone, although the second method was used most often.[7] Since our interviews already had each client's file (which included background information on the person, his or her family situation, and a detailed description of the past violence), the interviewers focused their questions, presented in appendix B, on events since the clients graduated from or left the program. In brief, they probed for various types of violence and strains that might have occurred since graduating or leaving the programs, how the persons or couples coped with these, and what they thought of the programs.

A major problem in longitudinal studies is that people move their residences frequently. Nationwide, one out of every four Americans relocates every year. It was the same in the population we studied. When the last known telephone numbers and addresses (and directory assistance) proved no help, our interviewers tried relatives, friends, and sometimes public utility companies for locations of the men. Only a handful, once found, refused to talk with us. Three men, we learned, had been killed in the interim—one by police in a drug raid, one in a barroom incident, and one by his wife—and several more were incarcerated in jails or prisons around the state.

Finally, as a further check on some of the versions of postcounseling violence or nonviolence that both men and women gave to our interviewers, we compared computerized police reports of domestic disturbance calls from the Austin Police Department with our lists of the Austin program's clients and spouses. These reports gave not only descriptions of incidents but also complete information on all persons involved, down to details such as the violent person's birthdate.

Our follow-up efforts netted a total of 148 men and 96 women (wives or girlfriends), or roughly one-half and one-third, respectively, of the total lists of clients we received from the three programs.[8] (While we have no way of knowing for sure whether the clients and their spouses who remained in Austin, Tyler, and Arlington were more or less violent than those who had moved away, there also is no reason to think that they were any different.) By a variety of avenues we were able to arrive at some reasonable idea of how much violence remained among known violent people who were counseled to stop this behavior.

Men's Violence before Counseling: What Men and Women Remembered

Men and women clearly have different recollections of the precounseling violence in their relationships. Table 6–1 presents the ways these men assaulted their wives and girlfriends and how often. This table also indicates how often child abuse, physical beating, or sexual abuse was involved. For

Table 6–1
Violent Behavior among Men before Entering a Counseling Program

	Male Abuser		Spouse/Girlfriend	
	N	%	N	%
Type of Violence				
Push or shove	89	69.9	71	84.5
Physical restraint	54	41.9	59	70.2
Slap	75	58.1	60	71.4
Hits	55	42.6	58	69.0
Chokes	23	17.8	34	40.5
Punches	44	34.1	36	42.9
Kicks	28	21.7	32	38.1
Burns	2	1.6	6	7.1
Hair pulling	27	20.9	41	48.8
Cuts	10	7.8	8	9.5
Threats to use weapon	22	17.1	27	32.1
Involuntary sex	12	9.3	18	21.4
Use of weapon	14	10.9	20	23.8
Other violence	34	26.4	29	34.5
Frequency of Violence				
Once	27	23.3	6	7.4
Once a month	21	18.1	17	21.0
2–3 times a month	15	12.9	13	16.1
Once a week	10	8.6	10	12.4
2–3 times a week	5	4.3	7	8.6
Daily	2	1.7	4	4.9
Other	36	31.1	24	29.6
Total	116	100.0	71	100.0
Violence toward Children				
Yes	29	24.0	32	36.0
No	92	76.0	57	64.0
Total	121	100.0	89	100.0
Type of Violence toward Children				
Physical	25	20.7	22	24.7
Sexual	1	0.8	0	0.0

Note: Persons may have responded to more than one item. The percentage is the number responding to that specific question.

example, only slightly more than two-thirds of the men remembered having pushed or shoved during an argument, while more than eight out of ten women remembered being pushed or shoved. Four out of ten men recalled physically restraining (holding down, tying up, or locking up) women, yet seven out of ten women stated they had been restrained at least once. The same was true for all types of violence, from the less serious forms such as slapping and hitting to the more lethal extremes such as choking, punching, kicking, burning, pulling by the hair, cutting, threatening to use a weapon, raping, and using a weapon. The men consistently reported less violence than did the women. Likewise, the men remembered having been violent less often than did the women. And we found the same general pattern among the small number of instances involving child abuse.[9]

Why do the men and women not remember the violence in the same way? We know that many of the men had been drunk when they hit or began hitting. Probably some simply do not recall clearly all the things they said or did. As one man, who later joined Alcoholics Anonymous while he was in counseling for his violence, said, "I know she said I did those things, and I must have, because the police arrested me, but I only remember getting mad. Not what I did. I was too flat out drunk."

Likewise, certain types of violence might have made more of an impression on the physically weaker victims (women) than on the men. Shoving is a classic example. Many men did not recall pushing the women during arguments, yet the women received bruises and sore necks from being knocked against furniture and walls. Further, as we saw earlier, many men have selective recall about violent incidents when they enter counseling. Certainly the stigma of having been hauled into court on charges of assaulting a woman does not make them eager to begin confessing their sins anew to counselors. At that time it is not unusual for them to minimize or rationalize their behavior. One aftereffect of the counseling experience may be that it makes some men even more sensitive (and therefore embarrassed) about their violence problem.

There is the possibility that some women exaggerated what had been done to them (that is, that the men who minimized were really more truthful than we are giving them credit for), but comparing the women's versions of what originally happened and the counselors' reports case by case makes this unlikely. The best reason for the differences in what they recalled of earlier violence is that some men still underestimated their violence because of a sense of lingering guilt or an inability to remember all their actions. At the same time, it is important to note that in the majority of cases men and women agreed on the extent of the men's violence problem before getting help, a definite sign that far fewer men now tried to excuse or evade the responsibility for their actions.

Men's Violence during Counseling: Did It Go Up or Down?

We asked men the direct question "Were you violent toward your partner while you were in the program?" We also asked the women who had been their wives or girlfriends at that time about violence. The results are shown in table 6–2 and reveal that several important things happen when violent men are provided with counseling.

First, slightly less than one-third of the men admitted to abusing wives or girlfriends while they were participating in one of the three programs, while roughly four in ten women claimed that the violence continued. Once again, the men tended to underestimate their violence compared to the women. Yet this finding alone lends only weak support to the folk wisdom that claims violence counseling initially produces stress in violent men and therefore contributes to a temporary increase in male anger, since more than two-thirds of the men and almost two-thirds of the women said there had been no further violence since the men started counseling.

Second, we were interested not only in knowing whether violence occurred once counseling began but also what type of violence it was. Here again the one prediction was that physical violence would again go up. Three times as many women (29 percent) as men (12 percent) reported that the physical violence continued, but they were a minority of the respondents. No man, and only two women in the entire study, recalled any sexual abuse happening during this time.

This does not mean that marital life is transformed instantly after men enter counseling. In some cases the women also have their own anger-control problems, which are little affected. Men who take their counseling sessions seriously sometimes spend more than a few nights walking their laps around

Table 6–2
Violent Behavior among Men in Counseling

	Male Abuser		Spouse/Girlfriend	
	N	%	N	%
Admitting Violence				
Yes	40	30.3	33	38.8
No	92	69.7	52	61.2
Total	132	100.0	85	100.0
Type of Violence				
Physical	16	12.1	25	29.4
Sexual	0	0.0	2	2.4
Total				

Note: Most, though not all, respondents answered questions on these specific points, hence Ns are not necessarily totals.

the block to wait until both they and their mates cool off. Initially some men do not share what they learn in counseling sessions with their partners, and this mistake can lead to misunderstandings. For example, one temperamental man and his equally hot-tempered wife were weeding their vegetable garden not long after he had been shown breathing and mental imagery anger-control exercises. During an argument, he abruptly sensed his own anger rising and walked off to a corner of their backyard, sat down cross-legged, and began a routine of slow breathing and counting down from 10. His wife had never seen this routine before and angrily paced back and forth, berating him for ignoring her while he was really trying to lower his blood pressure and anger potential. She was even angrier than before when he finally acknowledged her own rising voice. His error was that he had never discussed with her what he had been practicing in the counseling program.

It is true, as table 6–2 shows, that the numbers of men and women who reported violence were by no means large, but that is the point: For the majority (two-thirds) of couples, physical and sexual violence did not continue once the man entered a given counseling program. There was no evidence in any of these cases where violence recurred during the counseling period that the abuse (physical or sexual) was caused or made worse by counseling per se. Any violence that did occur seemed to be a continuation of precounseling problems. Thus for some men the counseling effect apparently does not take when they first start or later while they are still in the programs. For most men, however, it does.

Men's Violence after Completing Counseling: The Acid Test

The acid test of any anger-control program is finding out how much abuse of women still persists after men complete counseling. As yet there is no official success rate or any quota of nonviolent men that such a program must achieve to be judged effective. Nor has success ever been spelled out other than in vague terms such as the reduction of violence. This is the problem with most family violence programs, whether they serve men or women, victims or perpetrators. They do not clearly define when they have done their job. They rarely lay out criteria for success. What if a program were to take men who regularly and very violently batter women (for instance, kicking, choking, and threatening them with weapons) and helped bring their anger under enough control so that any later violence was rare and not more than slapping? Should we say it is a failure? What if a violent man learned to stop physically abusing his wife, but the couple still bickered or even sought divorce? Does success for such a program necessarily include making marriages and sexual relationships happier and more fulfilling, or will a program have done its job if physical and sexual violence cease?

In the absence of any clear guidelines to answer such questions, we reasoned that if a program is doing its job, then more men ought to be changed than not changed. That means we should expect a successful program to score better than 50 percent in affecting past habits of violence. Specifically, we would require that the following three standards be met by programs in order to judge them effective:

1. Most of the physical violence (that is, beatings and rapes) has to stop altogether.

2. When such violence does continue, it should be markedly reduced.

3. There should be accompanying side effects in the direction of making men's relationships with women more positive by however they themselves (particularly the women) define improvement.

These criteria probably seem, from the average person's viewpoint, altogether reasonable demands to make on such counseling programs. These programs, after all, usually charge their clients fees or ask community or state agencies for financial support. If all the trained personnel available, with their theories and experience, were unable to succeed more times than not, then why should they be supported or even allowed to operate?

Counselors, however, know that many other factors go into helping a client resolve any problem. The client's own motivation to be helped or change, the support of his or her network of immediate relatives and friends, the demands and strains of employment and everyday life all may work against the program's success. Such factors may be equally important, and any one could erode or even cancel out the counselor's efforts. The counselor frequently has little or no control over these.

We are satisfied to adopt these hard criteria because they are the ones that critics and persons suspicious of such anger-control programs frequently hold. The third criterion in particular—that programs designed to stop anger and violence also are to make intimates more compatible—make heavy demands on this counseling process. Nevertheless, until programs that counsel violent men can prove their effectiveness under the strictest circumstances and in the most hostile arenas, they will always meet a certain amount of resistance and even resentment. Therefore, we adopt these criteria for success.

Table 6–3 presents the results of our follow-up study of men who graduated from three anger-control programs in Texas. (As an adjunct, table 6–4 shows the frequency of postcounseling child abuse according to women respondents.) Among the 148 men we interviewed, 102 (or 69 percent) had completed these programs. It is this subgroup that we will use to evaluate the programs' effectiveness. Forty women related to these graduates served as independent sources of information on the postcounseling situation.

Table 6–3
Violent Behavior among Men after Completing a Counseling Program

	Male Abuser		Spouse/Girlfriend	
	N	%	N	%
Type of Violence[b]				
Physical	14	15.5	10	25.0
Sexual	2	2.2	2	5.0
Physical Violence[a]				
Less severe	11	12.2	7	17.5
Same	2	2.2	4	10.0
More severe	1	1.1	0	0.0
Sexual Abuse				
Less severe	1	1.1	1	2.5
Same	1	1.1	1	2.5
More severe	0	0.0	1	2.5
Frequency				
Once	5	5.5	6	15.0
Once a month	4	4.4	2	5.0
2–3 times a month	3	3.3	1	2.5
2–3 times a week	2	2.2	1	2.5
Daily	0	0.0	1	2.5
Other	11	12.2	9	22.5

Note: There is some inconsistency in information provided by the respondents. For example, only two women admitted to sexual abuse after their partners completed the program, but three women responded to the question about the severity of sexual abuse after the program. Data were not adjusted to correct these inconsistencies.

[a]A few men would not respond to this question.

[b]Some men and women reported committing more than one type of violence.

We asked men the question, "Have you been violent toward your partner since you completed the program?" and asked the women a similar one, "Has he been abusive or violent toward you since he completed the program?" Less than one man in five (or a total of sixteen of the men replied that they had been violent in some way, while twelve women (or one in four) reported being abused.

Our interviewers also asked both men and women whether any physical or sexual abuse that recurred had become less severe, more severe, or remained about the same as it was before counseling. Of the sixteen men who reported their own continued physical violence, eleven said it was less severe and only one man said it was more severe (and it was his wife's violence, he told us, not his). The statistics, as table 6–3 shows, follow the same pattern for sexual assault. Two men out of the entire group reported continued sexual abuse, and it had been either less severe or about the same as it had been earlier. Only one woman said it had become more severe. More importantly, only one man claimed that his postcounseling abuse was more severe. Almost all other men said that their continued violence was less

Table 6–4
Frequency Distribution of Postcounseling Child
Abuse According to Women Respondents

Questions on Child Abuse	Spouse/Girlfriend	
	N[a]	%
Any Abuse since Program		
Yes	6	12.5
Frequency		
Once	2	4.2
Once a month	2	4.2
2–3 times a month	1	2.1
2–3 times a week	1	2.1
Physical Abuse		
Yes	3	6.3
Sexual abuse		
Yes	1	2.1

[a]$N = 48$

severe. No woman claimed that the severity of physical abuse had increased; in fact, for most it had become less severe. And in almost every instance the frequency of violence had dropped off dramatically compared to precounseling days, even though in many cases these families were contacted a year, two years, or longer after the men had left counseling.

Table 6–5 shows the various issues over which anger arose in postcounseling violence and the actions both men and women took immediately afterward. There was no single reason why tempers flared and anger went out of control. Men and women cited the usual gamut of pressures: finances, jobs, sexual demands, alcohol and drug use, unemployment, raising children, and sexual jealousy. These are, as we noted earlier, factors that in many cases counselors can do little to affect.

After the violent relapse, both men and women took a variety of actions. Sometimes the man quickly recovered self-control and either discussed his lapse with his wife or left to take a walk and cool down. Sometimes she left, afraid once more. But according to the women interviewed, only ten of them felt enough of the old fear to call the police. Since many of them had been willing to do this before counseling began, this low figure reinforces what they told us earlier: When violence does recur, it is less severe, thus giving the women hope that it eventually can be controlled. Typical of such situations is how one housewife described continuing flare-ups of her husband's anger: "He's much better now at being able to stop being angry. Once in a while he leaves the house for a while (when his anger starts), but comes back OK."

In sum, these figures tell us several important things. First, physical and

Table 6–5
Factors That Contribute to Violence and Ensuing Actions

	Male Abuser		Spouse/Girlfriend	
	N	%	N	%
Factors				
Alcohol use	6	24.0	9	25.7
Drug use	2	8.0	2	8.6
Unemployment	2	8.0	3	8.6
Job pressures	5	20.0	10	28.6
Sexual demands	2	8.0	1	2.9
Financial pressures	7	28.0	8	22.9
Conflict over children	7	28.0	4	11.4
Conflict over other family members	3	12.0	3	8.6
Jealousy	7	28.0	4	11.4
Aggression by spouse	1	4.0	0	0.0
Other	9	36.0	12	34.3
Ensuing Actions				
Argument	14	48.3	7	20.0
Calm discussion	9	31.0	11	31.4
Abuser left house	5	17.2	6	17.1
Spouse left house	6	20.7	10	28.6
Called agency for advice	0	0.0	2	5.7
Spouse called other family member	1	3.4	5	14.3
Abuser called other family member	0	0.0	2	5.7
Called police	3	24.1	10	28.6
Other	7	24.1	10	28.6

Note: The total N varies as it refers to the persons responding to the question.

sexual violence stopped in the majority of cases (eight out of ten men versus seven out of ten women said it never recurred after counseling). This finding satisfies our first criterion for success in such programs–that is, that most of the violence has to stop completely.

Second, when violence did recur after the men graduated from these programs, it was almost always remarkably reduced, even by the victims' admissions. This finding satisfies our second criterion for success in such programs—that is, that remaining violence must be less serious and reduced.

Our third criterion for success in antiviolence programs must be met based on information that is outside any statistics on how often violence has stopped or decreased, however, and it is to such findings that we now turn.

Men's and Women's Lives after Counseling

Our third criterion for judging an anger-management or anger-control program's success requires not merely that violence cease or decrease but that men's and women's relationships with each other improve in other ways. Actually this is not such a stringent goal as it might seem since the counseling programs did more than simply try to stop violence. They also taught communication skills as well as the basic psychology of sex roles, and they provided other information designed to strengthen the underlying foundation of intimate adult relationships.

Critics of such programs who want sexist oppression made a more explicit and expanded part of counseling agendas (and who desire less psychology, since anything short of emphasizing sexism is seen as inadequately stopgap) claim that simply ending the violence is not enough. Battered women, they argue, often are terrorized by the anticipation or threat of battering as much as by the violence itself. Some abusive men, they correctly point out, eventually do not have to use violence to get their way because they can intimidate women who believe they are likely to batter. According to this logic, stopping the overt violence is no guarantee that the sexist oppression and abuse has really ended. The women, in other words, may still live in an atmosphere of fear and intimidation. One critique of our initial statistical findings from the follow-up project followed just such a line of argument:

> In the so-called successful cases, the women by trying harder to please, could have left the relationship . . . or might have threatened the men more with reprisals. . . . We really have no way of knowing why the men reduced the violence and what effect it has had on the women. The real question may be what personal changes the men have experienced, i.e., do they view women differently, are they less jealous, do they share decisions more, are the family finances distributed more evenly, does the man help with the housework at all, does he encourage his wife's ideas and visions rather than degrade them?[10]

One indirect measure of improvement in relations would be both men's and women's feelings about the programs in which either one or both of them participated. As table 6–6 shows, both men and women generally gave high marks to the programs' personnel and counselors. Eight out of ten males and more than seven out of ten women considered the personnel to be good or excellent. More importantly, eight out of ten men and more than six out of ten women felt that the programs had been either fairly helpful or very helpful to their particular problems. Almost all of the men believed that their counselors understood and addressed their problems. Perhaps most conclusive in summing up clients' general satisfaction with the programs is the fact that 98 percent of the men and 95 percent of the women said that they would recommend the programs to others with similar problems. (In fact, one criticism we frequently heard of all three programs from both men and women was that they needed to do more advertising in the community and expand facilities to take in more people who needed help.) Two-thirds of the women felt that the programs were fairly to very helpful

Table 6–6
Client Evaluations of Counseling Programs

Program Attribute	Male Abuser		Spouse/Girlfriend	
	N	%	N	%
Client Rating of Personnel				
Very poor	0	0.0	2	4.5
Poor	1	1.0	0	0.0
Good	18	18.4	9	20.5
Very good	34	34.7	15	34.1
Excellent	45	45.9	18	40.9
Total	98	100.0	44	100.0
How Helpful Was the Program				
Not at all helpful	1	1.0	5	11.1
Not very helpful	2	2.1	7	15.6
Somewhat helpful	15	15.6	4	8.9
Fairly helpful	19	19.8	9	20.0
Very helpful	59	61.5	2	44.4
Total	96	100.0	45	100.0
Clients in Counseling Previously	43	45.3	18	40.0
Clients Would Recommend Program to Others	93	97.9	41	95.3
Counselors Understood Problems	84	90.3	—	—
Client Knows Someone Who Could Benefit from Program	49	58.3	28	66.7

for them; the other one-third of the women saw that such counseling could help situations like theirs even if it had only been somewhat or a little helpful to them personally.

But the comments and anecdotes the women now living with nonviolent graduates told our (female) interviewers illustrated the more direct story. Many women expressed their relief that the men finally were able to control anger and violence. The consensus was that the men definitely had changed for the better. As one young woman put it "What he told me about his counseling sessions convinced me that it helped him get a handle on his temper." Another said, "He is embarrassed to admit it, but he not only benefitted from the program—he enjoyed it." Other women who had not been through counseling themselves nevertheless learned things from talking with their husbands about the therapy sessions. One housewife claimed, "Now I can use the skills I learned [from her husband] in everyday life, particularly with the children." Another said, "The program really showed us how to stay out of each other's way and avoid fights." One wife summed up this indirect benefit: "The man I know now and the man he used to be are totally different persons. Some of the things he learned have helped me!"

Women also elaborated on the other aspects of their relationships. Some women spoke frankly about how counseling had made the men better lovers in the general sense of opening up their sexual intimacy to freer communication and tenderness. One woman told a female interviewer, "Now we participate in our lovemaking as true equals. For the first time in our marriage, I feel satisfied and enjoy sex."

The men's ability to communicate more openly about their own needs and what they expect of women (which previously they could rarely articulate and therefore fueled their frustrations and hurt) is one significant improvement, according to their spouses and girlfriends. For example, consider the following sample of comments:

He really made a big change. He is now the ideal husband. He listens to what I say!

For the first time I feel like I am actually sharing in the relationship as a true partner.

I have more understanding from him now. I know more about our relationship.

The program helped our family to communicate better. Because of this, we haven't had any violence in our family at all since the program.

One Austin, Texas, woman admitted that her own violence problem had continued, but she nevertheless praised that city's men's antiviolence program.

Has he changed? Compared to the way he was with the way he is now— hell yes! He tries to understand my side of the argument. He talks to me rather than hits me. I still hit him, however. I would like to enroll in a class in anger management, but the [Austin] shelter for battered women does not help women with this problem.

In fact, many wives and girlfriends as well as many men complained that the Austin program in particular does not offer a parallel women's program. (It once did offer such services for victims and later revived these, but male and female counselors did not always see eye to eye on how to coordinate the complementary programs.)

A wife of an Austin man said that for him the love and caring shown by the staff had been the most important factor in changing his behavior. The personal attention he received began to rub off on the way he came to relate to her (that is, he began to identify with his counselors as role models).

In the Arlington program, where couples met in therapy sessions as a group, friendships and support networks developed. The program's director,

Dr. Jeanne Deschner, shared with us letters from graduates who wrote back to ask about favorite counselors and, significantly, about other clients. At one point a group of graduate couples even planned a reunion, and one woman wrote about her and her husband's regrets that his new job responsibilities prevented them from attending.

The men's receptivity to counseling and their willingness to correct their behavior (another index of success) also can be seen in their comments to male interviewers, who were careful to identify themselves as researchers evaluating the programs and not therapists. Many men wanted to see more expanded and diversified counseling formats. They thought that sessions should be held more than once a week, that the program should be geared to single men and even to gays, that counseling ought to be ongoing rather than for a limited time, and that refresher or booster sessions should be organized. One man suggested a children's anger-control program to catch the emerging problem closer to its source, and many men were quite emphatic that there should be a parallel women's program for their wives and girlfriends.

One ex-client whom we had seen at the first meeting of a group session at the Austin men's program said when we interviewed him one year later (after he had joined Alcoholics Anonymous), "It (the anger-control program) was the only thing that initially got me to stop drinking and save my marriage. There are still difficult times, but I'm still trying to earn her trust."

These are, obviously, the positive responses of successful graduates and the women with whom they lived. But the aftermath is not so saccharine for some women. Despite the fact that only twelve women said that counseling was not at all or not very helpful, we know that three in ten women continued to experience some sexual or physical violence, even if it was reduced. A few such women complained that the men lied to counselors and continued their violence or acted nonviolently for a while to get through the respective programs—the exact danger about which many feminist critics have warned. Most of these women had left men (separated or divorced) permanently. Men's violence has left too many emotional scars for them ever to consider continuing relationships that should be based on affection and trust. For them help simply came too late.

The Programs: What Worked?

The basic goal of the three programs in Austin, Arlington, and Tyler was the same: to end violence in families. As we have seen, counseling techniques used by the programs overlapped. All emphasized sex role reeducation, reality therapy, and what psychologists term cognitive structuring techniques. But there also were variations. Techniques of anger management, for example, ranged from sophisticated biofeedback to meditation and breathing exercises to role playing. The three programs also differed in their formats: men in all-male discussion sessions and individual counseling (Austin), couples alone with counselors (Tyler), and couples in groups with teams of counselors (Arlington). Yet when we compare the three shelters, it is not apparent that any of the different formats and counseling techniques is superior to the others. Each program significantly reduced or eliminated violence and in many cases produced happier as well as healthier (and safer) relationships between men and women.

On the one hand, such a finding is a little frustrating because we do not yet know which of the elements of each program were crucial to success and which were unimportant. How much of each program could be trimmed without sacrificing effectiveness? Conversely, what should be emphasized more? How much of the violence would be eliminated or changed, if at all? These are the sorts of more focused questions that future research must ask.

On the other hand, these results suggest that no one counseling format is indispensable and that programs probably have a range within which they can be organized and still have an impact. The three programs did, however, have similarities that we consider essential ingredients for family violence programs:

1. Holding the violent person personally responsible for his or her violent actions and stressing that he or she is not powerless to stop it.

2. Trying to get objective, independent information on the violent persons and monitoring whenever possible their behavior during the time they are in the counseling program.

3. Creating a moral atmosphere in counseling sessions that says physical violence and emotional abuse is not appropriate or excused. It is not macho or normal.

It may well be that screening men (and women) and convincing them, with the help of the courts or other professionals, that they have a serious problem likely to become more serious is more important than any specific litany of dos and don'ts for therapists. As we mentioned earlier in this chapter, two sociologists found that many of the men who had been arrested for assaulting women had stopped the beating and abusing without any counseling whatsoever.[11] Sociologist Edward Gondolf also did a follow-up study similar to ours on a smaller number of violent men who graduated from a Pennsylvania counseling program and discovered that men who had started but never finished counseling were as likely to have stopped abusing women as men who completed the program.[12] One tentative conclusion to be drawn from such studies is that official agencies confronting a violent man with irrefutable evidence that he has a problem has a significant impact on his behavior.

Thus in ways we are just beginning to understand, confronting violent men, who are otherwise of average intelligence, with the inappropriateness—both legal and moral—of their actions seems to work. The men's behavior and attitudes can be changed, to everyone's satisfaction.

There also may be some effect gained from having a man enter a counseling program, even if he does not finish it. Certainly the Gondolf study suggests this. We tried to interview men, and their girlfriends or wives, who had been terminated from the three Texas programs. Table 6–7 presents the results. These persons were more difficult to track down and often were curt, sullen, and generally uncooperative with interviewers. Some bluntly swore at us or firmly insisted that they had nothing to say, that we had no business asking them any questions, or that we should never call again. Certainly they were less open and cooperative than most of the graduates and their mates. Even though the numbers are smaller, the patterns are clear. We found more men admitting to physical violence (45 percent) than in the

Table 6–7
Violent Behavior among Men Not Completing Counseling Programs

	Male Abuser		Spouse/Girlfriend	
	N	%	N	%
Admitted Violence[a]				
Yes	13	44.8	20	66.7
No	16	55.2	10	33.3
Total	29	100.0	30	100.0
Type of Violence[b]				
Physical	5	17.2	15	50.0
Verbal	15	51.7	18	60.0
Sexual	1	3.4	1	3.3
Physical Violence				
Less severe	3	10.3	7	23.3
Same	0	0.0	5	16.7
More severe	3	10.3	5	16.7
Sexual Abuse				
Less severe	0	0.0	0	0.0
Same	0	0.0	2	6.7
More severe	0	0.0	0	0.0
Frequency				
Once	3	10.3	3	10.0
Once a month	3	10.3	3	10.0
2–3 times a month	0	0.0	3	10.0
2–3 times a week	1	3.4	3	10.0
Daily	0	0.0	3	10.0
Other	7	24.3	6	20.0

[a]A few men did not respond to this question.

[b]Some men and women reported committing more than one type of violence.

group of graduated (28 percent). Likewise, their spouses and girlfriends reported physical violence more often (67 percent) than did women related to the graduates (30 percent). Nevertheless, many of these men had not abused women since being terminated from their programs. And more of these women reported that the severity of physical violence had remained the same or decreased than said it had gotten worse.

Lastly, a check of computerized police reports from the Austin Police Department produced a total of eight men with the same names of men who had entered the city's Family Violence Diversion Network program, roughly at the rate of one every other month. As a source of independent validation, police statistics indicated relatively few callbacks to homes of men who were arrested and then counseled for assault.

Critics might say that the minority of women who still experienced violence had tried the criminal justice system and then counseling and had found them both ineffective. Thus these women did not bother to call the police again. This is a possibility, although most women reported that there were other ways they coped with subsequent violence. An equally plausible reason, given that we know physical violence almost always decreased after counseling if it is not eliminated altogether, is that these women found the violence more bearable. Perhaps they had more hope that it could end since they had seen it change once already. While such improvements might not be considered successes or victories by critics who want all traces of violence scourged from male psyches and American culture, these definitely were changes for the better in the homes of those couples.

But there is a limit to what counseling can do after the fact in a violent home. Some physical and emotional scars cannot be healed. This will be the case as long as we rely solely on intervention that waits for the abuse to start. In our final chapter we propose a more coordinated, anticipatory scheme of intervention, one that depends on the entire community rather than any single agency or set of counselors.

7

Antiviolence Strategies at the Community Level

If we can't get beyond the victims, then we'll never solve the family violence problem. We'll never do more than stick Band-Aids on these women and send them back out into a rotten world.
—John Patrick, antiviolence counselor, Tyler, Texas

I magine a physician in private practice. Over several weeks he notices more and more patients coming to his office complaining of the same symptoms: fever, nausea, and diarrhea. At first he diagnoses each case as flu and simply writes prescriptions to lower body temperatures, settle stomachs, and kill intestinal viruses. Gradually, however, he begins to notice a pattern. Not only has this sickness assumed epidemic proportions among his patients, but these patients all live within one general area of the community. Checking with his colleagues, he finds that all their patients showing identical symptoms also reside in the same neighborhoods as his own patients. Finally, our physician investigates conditions in that part of town and discovers that the drinking water supply has become contaminated by a break in nearby sewer lines. After city crews are dispatched to replace pipes and seal the break, the torrent of patients with the earlier symptoms suddenly disappears.

The physician in our example at first treated only the symptoms of the underlying problem, regarding each patient's complaints as unique to him or her. As time went by, however, the physician come to suspect that these patients shared a common problem and that something was systematically producing it. Eventually he no longer considered patients' illnesses in individual terms; rather, he saw them as a community problem. At that point he intervened at an entirely different level—the public health level—to change that part of the environment in which they lived.

The change in the physician's understanding of the epidemic in his community is analogous to the revolution now developing in how we are coming to recognize and treat the sources of family violence. In chapter 1 we divided the emerging perceptions of family violence into three phases dealing, respectively, with victims, perpetrators, and the family system as well as the societal context in which these all exist as a whole. The physician's concern with the symptoms of individuals was at the first phase. Clearly it was necessary for alleviating suffering, but it failed to do much about the causes. Only when he began to address the source and thought in terms of the entire context (or system) in which his patients became ill did he move on to later phases.

The systems approach to family violence emphasizes the interrelations of many factors producing it. For example, there is the immediate issue about which they are quarreling. Frequently such issues seem incredibly trivial or even absurd to outsiders: She did not cook a main dish he wanted that particular night, she wore the wrong color dress or the wrong perfume, she returned home from work fifteen minutes later than she had said she would, and so on. To most of us these would be at worst minor irritants but hardly the stuff worth physically assaulting anyone (much less arguing) over. In fact, such issues are what intimate combatants use as an excuse to fight. It takes little probing to find that there are deeper layers and past experiences that set the conditions and provide the motivations for violent behavior.

Our search for these underlying causes has led us to consider biological, psychological, cultural, and economic levels. For some violent men or couples one level is a more important factor than others. For example, few of the violent men we encountered had blood sugar disorders, brain dysfunctions, or other physical ailments that could be directly linked to their violent actions. The majority, however, had been drinking shortly before they became abusive and destructive. Alcohol, the great disinhibitor and clouder of judgment, clearly affected tempers and accelerated some violence, but it was not the cause of most men's anger.

At the psychological level many men had been raised in violent homes where one or both parents were abusive to them as well as to each other. Their fathers often were poorly equipped with parenting skills. They were dry wells of affection who were uninvolved in much of their sons' lives. This resulted in a great deal of dependence on the mothers, who were expected to be all things to the boys but yet never could be. As these boys grow into men, they come to transfer this style of emotional dependence on the women with whom they are married or live. Their domineering, exploitive, jealous control of the women, including physical beatings if the women rebel, actually are desperate acts to try to hold on to these love objects that can comfort their insecurity. Sadly, these men become less than adequate fathers themselves, passing on the risk of emotional shortcomings and dependence to their sons.

Many men, and not always those described above, saw their fathers quarrel violently with their mothers and now use physical strength to win (or silence) arguments and control households. Violence also can be a male strategy to deal with females, the success of which is learned on a regular, intimate basis.

The cultural level of sexism reinforces these violent actions and excuses them by making men's domination of women a virtue rather than a character flaw or vice. Macho men do not cry or display soft emotions, and they feel justified in lashing out at women who question their authority or control. Anger, in other words, is manly. Violence is a man's prerogative, not a problem of self-control. In this way such men are not encouraged to see their violence as anything needing help or to deal with their underlying insecurities. They see their violent acts as discrete, isolated incidents, not as a pattern, as their victims do. Sexism, in other words, provides the attitudes and beliefs that rationalize, support, and sanction their use of violence. It is no wonder that so many violent men deny that they have a serious problem and so rarely seek any type of counseling unless literally coerced into it by fed-up women or the law.

Their emotional feelings of dependence, combined with the traditional sex role of the United States' traditionally sexist culture, is the single greatest reason these men must be pressured to seek help. But as we also have seen, the cultural smoke screen includes more than just the notion that bigger, stronger men naturally should be the bosses of their weaker family members. In some cases, conservative Christian beliefs also reinforce traditional male beliefs about dominance by using biblical justification. In some occupations, particularly the military, there is a not-so-subtle pressure to perceive the man as the one who gives the orders and the woman as the one who follows without question. This same pressure also works against anyone reporting violence in military families until it becomes literally life threatening and often many times worse than the abuse in civilian families.

Add to these levels one of economic strains and pressures that affect everyone to some degree. These pressures might include an inconsistent economy, unemployment, and the heavy, impersonal bureaucracies that confront consumers and employees alike. The frustrations they generate cannot be easily relieved because no single person is responsible and blame cannot be tangibly assigned.

Finally, move beyond the violent man and deal with the entire family situation. In a number of cases discussed in chapter 3, some women are mirror images of violent men at many levels. Such women have their own personality needs and, because of violent pasts, a lack of anger control. They may have seen their mothers behave as violently toward their fathers as their fathers did toward their mothers. They have been raised in a culture that in myriad ways has taught them how at least to feign dependence and submission even if they do not buy the entire role. These women have been encouraged to blame themselves if their marriages or intimate relationships are not successful. Not just secular culture tells them this, but also some popular religions do. Economic pressures literally hit home when their impact is felt by all members of the family, whether they work or not.

Thus understanding any violent man, woman, or couple often is a matter of unraveling various tangled patterns of cause and effect. For a counselor each case before him or her is unique, yet as we have found, many violent people also share definite similarities. This fact makes counseling programs that can be set up to address certain standard violence problems feasible and useful. In the previous chapter we evaluated three such programs, each operating according to a different format, and yet found each valuable. Each program, however, went beyond a beginning concern with only the victims of family violence. These programs, and others like them, clearly show that sometimes there are violent women and violent couples, just as there are violent men, although women's violence appears to be much less frequent and severe. An exclusive focus on victims, therefore, becomes not just unrealistically narrow but also misleading. If communities are to deal effectively with family violence, they must develop a comprehensive approach that provides safety for victims, treatment and legal consequences for perpetrators, coordinated services for dysfunctional families, and societal changes that reduce the social norms and conditions that contribute to the problem.

The implications of the systems approach for how we treat family violence are obvious. For some families, simply counseling the men will not resolve their problems. Even in the majority of cases where the violence is always one-sided (male) and the victims are always women (and children), the men cannot be counseled in a vacuum because they do not live in a vacuum. Multimodal approaches and networking are needed for referrals, education, and counseling. Optimally, the female partner must be included in the counseling program, if only to understand for herself the dynamics of her partner's anger and what he must do to overcome them. In one recent study of 250 families in a counseling program in Suffolk, Virginia, researchers discovered that all those who remained in the full two-year program ceased their violence. Like the three programs we evaluated, a good number of the Suffolk program's marriages also were salvaged and improved by counseling. What was most significant, however, was that the researchers attributed the success to having both partners, victim and abuser, in the program together.[1]

Waiting for violence to erupt, for the victims to begin seeking safe havens and the perpetrators to begin filing into counseling, still represents symptomatic treatment at best. It is unquestionably necessary and valuable, but it also is intervention late in the process. The relatively few counseling programs for abusers are already strained to maximum capacity. Doubling or tripling their size would not take care of the large number of assault-prone people in even modest-sized communities.

We are in need of more comprehensive strategies for confronting family violence. Clinicians call this strategy secondary intervention, seeking out those areas of society and those subpopulations particularly at risk from the sociological and social psychological conditions that make violence more likely. In other words, we must lower the probability of violence by alerting key community gatekeepers to anticipate it rather than to sit back in counseling centers and women's shelters waiting for the body count to begin.

Implementing the Community Response

The lack of community response to family violence usually is explained by a chain of negativism in the criminal justice system. Abused female citizens do not call the police because either the abusive men calm down soon after violent incidents or they have called the police in the past and the police failed to respond or did not arrest. Police in turn do not arrest perpetrators of violence because often (1) the turbulent scene has quieted by the time they arrive; (2) the woman has changed her mind and balks at pressing assault charges; or (3) if she does press charges, she must deal with a variety of social pressures, mixed emotions, and sometimes threats of further violence and intimidation, which contribute to her often dropping charges. Overworked prosecutors, who live by the professional standard of winning cases (and who therefore tend to prosecute only winnable cases), do not choose to prosecute domestic assault cases because of the gray (rather than black and white) nature of family violence. Like the police, they also point to the many women who press charges but later back out for emotional or economic reasons. Finally, judges face court dockets that already are overcrowded, may not be well informed about family violence, and in some cases still regard it as a civil or domestic, rather than a criminal, matter. The family violence problem, in other words, is perceived as a no-win situation at each step of the criminal justice system.

In larger society similar problems work against eliminating family violence. In both the military and churches, as we have shown, important institutions that affect millions of Americans can contribute (if inadvertently) to the problem. Until recently the military wife (and family) was regarded by every branch of the service as an appendage not to be factored into the upholding of military morale and readiness. Likewise, most clergy have had little or no exposure to the social scientific knowledge about family violence, even if they studied pastoral counseling during seminary training. (And in many Protestant groups clergy are called to their profession by inspiration rather than entering through the paths of formal education.)

Similarly, the medical education of doctors and nurses concentrates on injuries and hurt in general, not on victims of assault in particular. Professional training for public school teachers is thin enough on substantive courses so that they must rely on intuition rather than systematic preparation in recognizing the telltale signs of abused children or mothers. Psychiatrists and psychologists in private practice, unless they have sought out refresher courses in the family violence phenomenon, may not recognize a family violence problem as such. Rather, working within their own theoretical models, they may regard hostility and aggression simply as symptoms of sexual maladjustment, childhood dilemmas with sibling relationships, or some other intrapsychic maladaptation. Even public mental health officials can miss family violence's significance, focused as they are on more seriously disturbed persons who are leaving, entering, or in danger of entering mental institutions.

The unpleasant truth is that the gatekeepers and professionals of most communities are poorly prepared to be mobilized for antiviolence efforts. They often are not sufficiently aware of the problem, nor are they part of networks that can address the problem from many different fronts.

But several communities currently are providing state-of-the-art models for dealing with family violence and spouse abuse and generally conform to the ideal systems approach we endorse.

The Family Violence Diversion Network, a program of the Child and Family Service of Austin, Texas, began on September 1, 1981. (See chapter 2 for a description of its counseling program.) It emerged out of contacts, discussions, and meetings among a number of staff persons in agencies that regularly deal with different aspects of family violence. These agencies included the Austin Police Department (Victim Services), a municipal judge, Child and Family Service, the Austin Stress Clinic, and the city and county attorney's offices, as well as representatives from a total of fifteen community agencies and advocacy groups. Those and other agencies that handle rape crisis, child abuse, and legal aid all confronted family violence cases fairly often, but there was a sense that these services still were not getting to the source of violence. One police psychologist recalls,

> We realized that a hole existed in the services available for violent families. That hole was that no services existed to help men who batter their spouses or girlfriends. Not only did services not exist, but no leverage existed to encourage the men to seek counseling.[2]

Not only were men's services virtually nonexistent, but there also was a great deal of frustration among the professionals. Women's advocates saw nothing being done to discourage or reform abusive men through the legal system; the police were frustrated at returning to the same homes repeatedly as well as expending great time and expense on domestic disturbance calls; some judges were seeing the revolving door pattern of many such cases; and most counselors acknowledged that abusive men were notoriously resistant to entering counseling.

An initial task force grew out of these meetings, and the Family Violence Diversion Network was the result. It operated (and still operates) through a court-diversion and court-mandated system, as we described briefly in chapter 2. (It is interesting to note that the number of volunteer or wife-mandated men has increased steadily since its inception.) There are a number of criminal justice system routes that an abusive man can take into the program, which is initiated when a woman files assault charges. He may enter by a six-month deferred adjudication, as a condition of probation, a plea bargain, or a protective order. In the case of serious or repeated abusers, care must be taken because the rehabilitation needed may be far greater than the counseling provided by the program. Even if admitted, such men must have close monitoring by counselors and law enforcement agents. The U.S. Commission on Civil Rights recommended diversion programs for moderately abusive men who do not have serious violent or criminal pasts:

> In cases where the pattern of abuse has not yet resulted in serious injury, and where abusers genuinely desire to alter their behavior and have the additional motivation of incarceration for failure to do so, counseling may help them learn how to handle stress without resorting to violence. Where defendants are charged with serious or repeat offenses, mandatory counseling is an insufficient sanction.[3]

Close cooperation between diversion programs and the criminal justice system is mandatory to ensure safety for women and children and to provide consequences to men who drop out of the program or continue to abuse their partners. This monitoring will demonstrate to the latter, their partners, and their friends that family violence is a criminal matter that will be taken seriously by all concerned. This is a mechanism by which society, through its official agents, states clearly and unequivocally that violent domineering behavior is wrong and will not be tolerated.

A critical ingredient of some programs, including the Austin diversion network, is the no-drop rule adopted by the courts and the prosecuting attorneys. This policy is put into effect to remove the decision to drop charges from the hands of abused women. Before the task force's commitment to no-drop policies, about half of the assault charges against husbands and boyfriends were dropped. Currently, once assault charges are filed, the prosecutor as an agent of the state chooses to pursue prosecution of the case. Again, this tells both parties that filing a criminal charge is a serious matter and will be prosecuted as such.

In this way the police are more likely to respond to domestic disturbance calls because they know if they arrest a man, it will not be simply a revolving door situation. The wife cannot arbitrarily drop assault charges once they are filed. And the police have confidence that their efforts spent on such arrests will be taken seriously by prosecutors. Likewise, prosecutors are more willing to take such cases into court because they know judges will not simply dismiss them as frivolous family squabbles. Judges, in turn, have the diversion option to move assault cases quickly through their courts with the expectation that the chances of the same man reappearing on the same charge will be markedly diminished.

A skeptic might wonder whether the no-drop rule would deter some women from calling police or filing assault charges, knowing they cannot back out once the legal process is set in motion. This does not seem to be the case. Calling the police rarely is a calm, rational decision: Women are emotionally distraught, frightened, and frequently in pain when they telephone for help. Many later have told us that they actually felt relieved when they learned that filing the charges was irreversible. They could report to their husbands that they had tried to have charges dropped but that the police would not cooperate. The blame and responsibility for the men's court appearances were then shifted away from the women, and an important point was reaffirmed in the minds of all involved: Filing criminal charges against persons is a serious police matter, not to be done or undone lightly.

From the standpoint of mobilizing the criminal justice component and related sectors of the community, two important aspects of the Austin model must be emphasized. First, rather than frustration, every agency or group of actors in the system gets something positive out of this arrangement. It makes their jobs easier and more effective, an incentive for any professional. In fact, the arrangement must satisfy the interests of all involved, or no one will be motivated to cooperate for very long.

Second, this sort of arrangement, put together and promoted by a task force, is the product of an unofficial umbrella group that has no formal power. Its individual representatives do, however, have clout within their respective organizations, and it is there that they can take steps to implement changes desired by the task force.

A prime example has been the use of protective orders. The Texas Family Code provides an inexpensive way for an abused woman to take out a court of protection (order) on a violent man that can restrict him (under threat of arrest) from coming within 200 yards of her place of residence or place of business and prohibits harassing communications and committing family violence. The cost is a nominal fee (differing across jurisdictions but frequently less than $20), and the woman is supposed to be able to obtain such a protective order from the county in minimum time and with few bureaucratic complications.

In reality the system was fraught with red tape, misinformation, confusion, and undefined responsibilities. There also was lax enforcement of protective orders, since even if the abusive man did violate one, individual police officers knew nothing about it when they answered disturbance calls. The orders had not even been entered into the police computer.

The task force streamlined the process by identifying the problems in filing such orders as well as their logistics and enforcement. As a result the county attorney appointed an assistant county attorney to oversee the judicial process of filing and adjudication. A county judge took a personal interest in educating and encouraging clerks to meet the requirements of the law. Police representatives took responsibility for making sure orders were entered on the computer as soon as possible, thereby making enforcement a more realistic outcome when an order was violated. The women's shelter representative increased the flow of information to battered women about the availability of this legal option, and judges' courts routinely ordered more men into counseling as part of protective orders.

In addition to the involvement of professionals such as those we have described, an ideal systems approach would include many more sectors of the community and attached gatekeepers, such as physicians, nurses, public mental health professionals, public school officials and teachers, journalists and other media professionals, and representatives from the business community and employee assistance programs. With broader cross-sections of the community involved, such task forces can not only overcome systematic obstacles related to family violence services but also set agendas of primary intervention, such as increasing community awareness that family violence is not only a significant social ill but also a crime that costs Americans millions (perhaps billions) of dollars each year. Part of this awareness would be the understanding that this violence is eroding the foundations of American family life and threatening a future generation of adults. Such objectives obviously are long-term undertakings that will call on the expertise of the entire community and employ all available means of communication, legal statutes, and a diverse set of advocates.

An innovative approach being used in Austin is to identify alleged perpetrators and their victims through public records of family disturbance calls responded to by the police department. These individuals receive a letter that gives information on family violence and appropriate counseling agencies. Brochures from the local battered women's shelter and men's counseling program also are provided.

Workshops and lectures for hospital staffs, public school counselors, and clergy can have a trickle-down effect aimed at primary intervention. The process is slow, however, and there are still real difficulties caused by the limited number of persons in the community who have the expertise (and time) to help educate the public. That is undoubtedly the greatest challenge to the broader mandate of primary intervention. It requires greater resources, and involves many more people of diverse skills, than do programs that counsel only the casualties of family hostilities. Yet the outcomes would be, by virtually everyone's account, more than worth the investment.

Confronting the Violent Society: A Final Word

Many citizens have become concerned about spreading instances of violence, but unfortunately their responses to these have been more on the order of hysteria than of reason. The difference between hysteria and reasonable response is one of thoughtful perspective. Hysteria is fueled by panic. It occurs when an imminent threat is seen, and then, out of intense fear, some quick or immediate solution is eagerly sought. Reasonable response asks more of any solution being offered. Is the purported solution realistic? Is it long term rather than some fly-by-night panacea?

Hysterical solutions for violence abound in our society. We have seen women in our own Texas communities flock to local karate schools or invest in kung fu lessons at the YWCA every time the local news reports a woman's having been kidnapped or raped. Some people arm themselves to the teeth or turn their homes into electronically sealed encampments. On the wall outside one of our own classrooms the university allowed the posting of a sign (obviously targeted at coeds) reading, "You can't rape 40,000 volts." It was a commercial advertisement for an electric stun gun complete with battery and charger (and had been approved for posting by the school administration).

Marcia Nutter lives in Fort Worth, Texas. She is an author, black belt in karate, and a longtime worker in the rape-prevention movement. She told us that in her experience she has found an understandable but widespread illusion among many women that there is some instant recipe or marvelous secret that will remove the threat and fear of violence. Once the touted answer was a can of Mace. Recently, in this high-tech age, it has become stun guns and simplistic six-week courses in hand-to-hand combat. In the lives of the violent couples we studied, the same dream panacea was the desperate hope of many women (and some men) that simply going to church or attending counseling would make their violence problem evaporate.

This type of short-term response to violence is symptomatic of the larger problem confronting our society. Instead of mounting a collective attack on general violence, we are letting it poison our sense of community. We are slowly fragmenting as communities in the face of it rather than pulling together. We are allowing distrust and paranoia to replace cooperation and determination. Citizens seem to be turning inward, pessimistically adapting a garrison mentality that accepts a certain amount of violence as part of a hopelessly deteriorating situation.

This attitude can result in a self-fulfilling prophecy in society at large, for if people abandon all but the most atomistic strategies for coping with violence ("I have my stun gun. Do you have yours?"), then they will most probably have to deal with violence solely on their own in the vigilante style

Appendix A
Life Endangerment Index

The Life Endangerment Index was constructed because certain forms of physical violence are life-threatening and therefore must be considered separately from less dangerous acts. Life-endangering forms of abuse in military families are choking, use of a weapon, and other. Other is used as an indicator of such danger because the abusive acts counted in this category included things such as smothering, amputation, starvation, and drugging. At the same time we realize that non-life-endangering abuse (such as broken glasses, pulled hair, and bruises) sometimes can lead to the death of a woman. For instance, verbal abuse alone could lead to suicide or sexual abuse to internal hemorrhaging.

Scoring for the two types of abuse was done in the following way:

1. Non-life-endangering behavior = 1
   Any life-endangering behavior = 2
2. Non-life-endangering injuries = 1
   Any life-endangering injury = 2

The men's scores on these two items were summed and a Life Endangerment Index score was assigned. The score for each man ranged from 1 to 4, with the values represented by the following:

Non-life-endangering = 1

Life-endangering = 2

Severely life-endangering = 3

Dangerously life-endangering = 4

Appendix B
Survey Instrument Used in Follow-up Study of Violent Men

Appendix B presents only the men's version of our interview schedule. Women were asked identical questions except on the subject of violence. Whereas the men were asked to describe their own postcounseling violence, the women were asked to describe the men's behavior.

MEN

Demographics and Case History
Date Entered _____

Date Left _____

City _____

1. Respondent's name (or I.D. #) _____

2. Age (in years) _____

3. Ethnicity:
   1. White _____
   2. Black _____
   3. Hispanic _____
   4. Other (specify) _____

4. Marital status while in program:
   1. Married _____
   2. Married but separated _____
   3. Widowed _____
   4. Divorced _____
   5. Cohabitating _____
   6. Single and not living together _____
   7. Single, none of the above circumstances _____

5. Current marital status:
   1. Married ____
   2. Separated ____
   3. Widowed ____
   4. Divorced ____
   5. Cohabitating ____
   6. Single and not
      living together ____
   7. Single, none of the
      above circumstances ____

6. How long have you been in this relationship?
   1. Months ____
   2. Years ____
   3. Don't know ____

7. Is this the same partner you had while you were in the program?
   1. Yes ____
   2. No ____

8. How many times have you been married? ____
   Your current partner? ____

9. How many children do you have? ____

10. How many children are living with you now? ____

11. Are these children: (check all that apply)
    1. Your natural children ____
    2. Your stepchildren ____
    3. Other

12. Formal education: Check highest level of education obtained.
    1. Less than high school ____
    2. High school diploma or GED equivalence ____
    3. 2-year college degree/some college ____
    4. 4-year bachelor's degree ____
    5. Vocational/technical school diploma ____
    6. Master's degree ____
    7. Doctorate degree ____

13. Current employment status:
    1. Employed ____
    2. Unemployed __
    3. Student ____
    4. Homemaker ____
    5. Other (specify)
       _____

14. If employed, briefly describe what you do. _____

15. How long have you been in your present job?
    Years _____ Months _____

16. How many different employers have you had in the past 5 years? _____

17. What is your total family income?
    1. $5,000 or less _____   5. $20,001–$25,000 _____
    2. $5,001–$10,000 _____   6. $25,001–$35,000 _____
    3. $10,001–$15,000 _____   7. More than $35,000 _____
    4. $15,001–$20,000 _____   8. Don't know _____

18. How long had the violence toward your partner been occurring before you entered the program? _____

19. Types of violence that occurred:
    1. Pushes/shoves _____   8. Burns _____
    2. Physical restraint _____   9. Hair pulling _____
    3. Slaps _____   10. Cuts _____
    4. Hits _____   11. Threats to use a weapon _____
    5. Chokes _____   12. Involuntary sex _____
    6. Punches _____   13. Other (specify) _____
    7. Kicks _____   14. Use of weapon or object _____

20. How often had the violence been occurring?
    1. Once _____   4. Once a week _____
    2. Once a month _____   5. 2–3 times a week _____
    3. 2–3 times a month _____   6. Daily _____
                                    7. Other (specify) _____

21. Was there any violence directed toward children or other family members?
    1. Yes _____   2. No _____

22. Was this violence: 1. Physical _____ 2. Verbal _____ 3. Sexual _____

Program Evaluation

23. How did you hear about the counseling program?
    1. Television/radio _____   7. Relative _____
    2. Newspaper/magazine _____   8. Church _____
    3. Friend _____   9. Partner _____
    4. Lawyer _____   10. Shelter for battered
    5. Police _____   women _____
    6. Court _____   11. Other _____

24. Under what conditions did you enter the program?
    1. Voluntary, through self-referral ____
    2. Voluntary, through other agency or professional agency ____
    3. Through court diversion, preplea ____
    4. Through court diversion, postplea ____
    5. Joint agreement between partner and myself ____
    6. Other (specify) _____

25. What type of format did your program use: (check all that apply)
    1. Group discussion ____   5. Family counseling ____
    2. Individual counseling ____   6. Family groups ____
    3. Couples counseling ____   7. Crisis-oriented counseling ____
    4. Couples groups ____   8. Other (specify) _____

26. What kinds of methods do you recall being used in your program? (check all that apply)
    1. Anger management ____
    2. Assertiveness training ____
    3. Building social support systems ____
    4. Communication skills training ____
    5. Drug alcohol intervention or treatment ____
    6. Emotional awareness training ____
    7. Emotional expression training ____
    8. Exploration of sex roles ____
    9. Problem solving skill training ____
    10. Role playing ____
    11. Stress management ____
    12. Support outside sessions
        (such as hotline access to program personnel) ____
    13. Tests/evaluations ____
    14. Other (specify) _____

27. How long were you in the program? Weeks ____ Months____

28. Did you finish the program? 1. Yes ____ 2. No ____

29. If you did not finish the program, what were your reasons? (check all that apply)
    1. Did not feel it was effective ____
    2. Did not like the personnel at the program ____
    3. Did not feel I needed it ____
    4. Times conflicted with job ____
    5. Other (specify) _____

30. Were you violent toward your partner while you were in the program?
    1. Yes _____   2. No _____

31. If yes, was it: 1. Physical _____   2. Verbal _____   3. Sexual _____

32. Have you been violent toward your partner since you left/completed the program? 1. Yes _____   2. No _____ (if no, go to question 40)

33. If yes, in what ways have you been violent? (check all that apply)
    1. Physical _____   3. Sexual _____
    2. Verbal _____   4. Other (specify) _____

34. If this violence was physical violence, has it been:
    1. Less severe _____   2. More severe _____   3. About the same _____

35. If this violence was verbal, has it been:
    1. Less severe _____   2. More severe _____   3. About the same _____

36. If this violence was sexual, has it been:
    1. Less severe _____   2. More severe _____   3. About the same _____

37. How many times have you been violent toward your partner since leaving the program?
    1. Once _____   5. 2–3 times a week _____
    2. Once a month _____   6. Daily _____
    3. 2–3 times a month _____   7. Other (specify) _____
    4. Once a week _____   _____

38. What do you think started the last abusive incident?
    Which of the following were associated with the last abusive incident against your partner or family member? (check all that apply)
    1. Alcohol use _____   7. Conflicts about or with child-
    2. Drug use _____   ren _____
    3. Unemployment _____   8. Conflicts about or with in-laws
    4. Job pressures _____   or other family members _____
    5. Sexual demands _____   9. Jealousy _____
    6. Financial or money   10. Other (specify) _____
       pressures _____   11. Physical aggression by your
                                        partner (describe) _____

39. What happened after the incident? (check all that apply)
    1. Argument _____
    2. Calm discussion _____
    3. You left the house/apartment _____
    4. She left the house/apartment _____
    5. Called agency for advice _____
    6. She called other family member _____
    7. You called other family member _____
    8. Called police _____
    9. Other (specify) _____
    10. Filed charges _____

40. How would you rate the program personnel?
    1. Very poor _____   3. Good _____   5. Excellent _____
    2. Poor _____   4. Very good _____

41. Would you recommend this program to others?
    1. Yes _____   2. No _____

42. How helpful do you think the program was?
    1. Not at all helpful _____   4. Fairly helpful _____
    2. Not very helpful _____   5. Very helpful _____
    3. Somewhat helpful _____

43. Do you think your counselors understood your specific problems?
    1. Yes _____   2. No _____   3. Don't know _____

44. Have you ever been in counseling or therapy before?
    1. Yes _____   2. No _____   3. Don't know _____

45. What factor or factors contributed to your decision to enter counseling?

    _____

46. Do you know someone personally that could benefit from this type of program?
    1. Yes _____   2. No _____   3. Don't know _____

47. In what ways do you think the program can be improved? _____

    _____

Notes

Chapter 1
Domestic Violence: The Evolving Problem

1. "Berkeley School Board OK's Domestic Violence Program," *Fort Worth Star-Telegram*, 23 August 1984.

2. News Release, New York State Department of Social Services, Albany, NY, 9 October 1984.

3. " 'Vision' Gives NBC Win in Ratings Race," *Fort Worth Star-Telegram*, 28 November 1984.

4. "Movie Spurs Calls to Shelters," *Fort Worth Star-Telegram*, 10 October 1984.

5. "Detective Ties Shooting to Show," *Fort Worth Star-Telegram*, 10 October 1984.

6. "Woman Who Set Spouse on Fire Hoping to Start Her Life All Over," *Fort Worth Star-Telegram*, 10 October 1984.

7. See "Man Attempted to Save Wife He Set on Fire, Neighbor Says," *Fort Worth Star-Telegram*, 10 October 1984; and "Woman Burned After Movie Dies," *Fort Worth Star-Telegram*, 16 October 1984.

8. William A. Stacey and Anson Shupe, *The Family Secret: Domestic Violence in America* (Boston: Beacon Press, 1983), 157.

9. *Attorney General's Task Force on Family Violence* (Washington, DC: U.S. Government Printing Office, 1984).

10. "War Urged Against Family Violence," *Fort Worth Star-Telegram*, 20 September 1984.

11. See *Parade Magazine*, 16 October 1983, 8; and "Dickey Charged With Beating Wife," *Fort Worth Star-Telegram*, 27 November 1984.

12. Michael Zielenziger, "Laws Get Tough on Home Violence," *Fort Worth Star-Telegram*, 2 December 1984.

13. Personal correspondence from Justice Norman E. Joslin, Supreme Court Chambers, State of New York, to Dr. A. David Shupe, 18 May 1984.

14. David Margolick, "Expert Testimony on Abuse Ruled Admissible to Show Self-Defense," *Fort Worth Star-Telegram*, 25 July 1984.

15. "Battered Wife Awarded $2.3 million," *Fort Worth Star-Telegram*, 26 June

1985; also see Nat Hentoff, "Police Pay Price for Failing to Protect Battered Wives," *Fort Worth Star-Telegram,* 1 August 1985.

16. *State of Texas* vs. *Tina Moffet,* August, 1984. Dallas, Tx.

17. Thomas S. Kuhn, *The Structure of Scientific Revolutions* 2d ed. (Chicago: The University of Chicago Press, 1970).

18. R. Emerson Dobash and Russell P. Dobash, "Wives: The 'Appropriate' Victims of Marital Violence," *Victimology: An International Journal* 2, nos. 3 and 4 (1977–78), 426.

19. Stacey and Shupe, *The Family Secret,* 11–12.

20. Terry Davidson, "Wifebeating: A Recurring Phenomenon Throughout History," in Maria Roy, ed., *Battered Women: A Psychosocial Study of Domestic Violence* (New York: Van Nostrand Reinhold, 1977), 14.

21. Elizabeth Pleck, "Wife Beating in Nineteenth-Century America." *Victimology: An International Journal* 4, no. 1 (1979), 61.

22. Susan Schechter, *Women and Male Violence* (Boston: South End Press, 1982).

23. Ibid., 55–56.

24. Keynote address by Susan Schechter to the Second Annual Texas Council on Family Violence Conference, Austin, TX, October 19–21, 1983.

25. Susan Schechter, *Women and Male Violence,* 42.

26. See Melissa J. Eddy and Toby Meyers, *Helping Men Who Batter: A Profile of Programs in the U.S.* (Austin, TX: Texas Department of Human Resources, 1984).

27. Susan Schechter, *Women and Male Violence,* 260.

28. Ibid., 261.

29. Barbara Hart, Memorandum entitled "Assessment of Counseling Programs for Men Who Batter," Pennsylvania Coalition Against Domestic Violence, 1984.

30. Schechter, *Women and Male Violence,* 3.

31. See Suzanne K. Steinmetz, "The Battered Husband Syndrome," *Victimology: An International Journal* 2, nos. 3 and 4 (1977–78), 499–509; and Murray A. Straus, Richard J. Gelles, and Suzanne K. Steinmetz, *Behind Closed Doors: Violence in the American Family* (Garden City, NY: Doubleday, 1980), 32.

32. See Erin Pizzey, *Scream Quietly or The Neighbors Will Hear* (Short Hills, NJ: Ridley Enslow Publishers, 1977); and Erin Pizzey and Jeff Shapiro, *Prone to Violence* (Middlesex, England: The Hamlyn Publishing Group, Ltd., 1982), 17–18.

Chapter 2
The Violent Man

1. "SEC Official Resigns After Disclosures," *Dallas Times Herald,* 27 February 1985, 1, 8A. See also "Woman Puts Abuse Behind Her, Rebuilds Character," *Fort Worth Star-Telegram,* 28 February 1985.

2. "DC Wives Unlikely to Report Beatings," *Fort Worth Star-Telegram,* 11 July 1979.

3. For recent examples, see Bruce J. Rounsaville, "Theories in Marital Violence; Evidence From a Study of Battered Women," *Victimology: An International*

Journal 3, nos. 1 and 2 (1978), 11–13; Bonnie E. Carlson, "Battered Women and Their Assailants," *Social Work* 22 (November 1977), 455–60; Mildred Daley Pagelow, *Women-Battering: Victims and Their Experiences* (Beverly Hills, CA: SAGE Publications, 1981); Elaine Hilberman and Kit Munson, "Sixty Battered Women," *Victimology: An International Journal* 2, nos. 3 and 4 (1978), 460–70; and William A. Stacey and Anson Shupe, *The Family Secret: Domestic Violence in America* (Boston: Beacon Press, 1983).

4. Examples would include Jeanne P. Deschner, *The Hitting Habit: Anger Control for Battering Couples* (New York: The Free Press, 1984); Richard J. Gelles, *The Violent Home* (Beverly Hills, CA: SAGE Publications, 1974); and D.G. Saunders, "A Model for the Structured Group Treatment of Male-to-Female Violence," *Behavior Group Therapy* 2 (1980), 2–9. The largest survey of violent males directly identified and interviewed appeared in Murray Straus, Richard Gelles, and Suzanne K. Steinmetz, *Behind Closed Doors: Violence in the American Family* (Garden City, NY: Press/Doubleday, 1980). These authors interviewed a cross-section of 2,143 Americans, half men and half women, to find that 16 percent of the couples contacted had used at least one form of violence in the home during the previous year. Husband abuse as well as wife abuse was discovered, and interviewees often did not seem loathe to discuss various aspects of their violence. These researchers' emphasis was more on frequency and types of violent incidents than on the more in-depth background of such violence that we probe for here.

5. "Wife Beating: The Silent Crisis," *Time* (26 September 1983).

6. More detailed descriptions of these programs and of the methods used to study them can be found in William A. Stacey and Anson Shupe, *An Evaluation of Three Programs for Abusive Men in Texas* (Austin, TX: Texas Department of Human Resources, 1984).

7. These case histories formed the core of our previous book, *The Family Secret*. Readers are referred to that source for further information on such violence victims.

8. Ibid., 96.

9. Ibid., 83.

10. Ibid., 86.

11. Jeanne P. Deschner, *The Hitting Habit*, 51.

12. The psychiatric instrument from which these statements were taken is called the SCL 90 and is comprised of ninety items, divided into five scales, that probe for signs of neurotic and psychotic symptoms. We have selected here a sample of the questions that have the least need of psychiatric interpretation. Future studies usually will clear up such mysteries. In this instance, however, the full disclosure of information that could answer the questions raised currently is handicapped by two important factors: (1) the lack of systematic statistical gathering and analysis of such information by military personnel, and (2) the unwillingness of many high-ranking military personnel—for public relations reasons or whatever—to open the entire matter to research and public inspection. Until both conditions are reversed, taxpayers and civilian citizens will have little meaningful idea of the true extent of military family violence or of what is effectively being done to address it.

Chapter 3
The Violent Woman

1. Murray A. Straus, Richard Gelles, and Suzanne K. Steinmetz, *Behind Closed Doors: Violence in the American Family* (Garden City, NY: Doubleday, 1980), 32.

2. Suzanne K. Steinmetz, "The Battered Husband Syndrome," *Victimology: An International Journal* 2, nos. 3 and 4 (1977–1978), 499–509.

3. Marvin E. Wolfgang, "Husband-Wife Homicides," *Corrective Psychiatry and Journal of Social Therapy* 2 (1976), 263–71.

4. *Texas Crime Victim Clearinghouse News,* 2 (Spring 1985), 2.

5. These data were collected in a study of courtship (premarital) violence among college students. See Richard N. Breen, "Premarital Violence: A Study of Abuse Within the Dating Relationships of College Students," unpublished master's thesis, The University of Texas at Arlington, May 1985, 49–65.

6. See, for example, William A. Stacey and Anson Shupe, *The Family Secret: Domestic Violence in America* (Boston: Beacon Press 1983), 90–94. See also Erin Pizzey, *Scream Quietly or The Neighbors Will Hear* (Short Hills, N.J.: Ridley Enslow Publishers, 1977) and R. Emerson Dobash and Russell P. Dobash, "Wives: The 'Appropriate' Victims of Marital Violence." *Victimology: An International Journal* 2, nos. 3–4 (1977–78), 426–47.

7. For a discussion of the generational transfer hypothesis and relevant research, see William A. Stacey and Anson Shupe, *The Family Secret: Domestic Violence in America* (Boston: Beacon Press, 1983), 41–46, 90–101.

8. Ibid., 122–27.

9. Robert Geffner, John Patrick, and Carol Mantooth, "Psychological Characteristics of Men and Women in Violent Relationships," paper presented at the annual meeting of the American Psychological Association, Toronto, Canada, August 1984.

Chapter 4
Family Violence in the Military

1. Nancy L. Goldman, "Trends in Family Patterns of U.S. Military Personnel During the 20th Century," in Nancy L. Goldman and David R. Segal, eds., *The Social Psychology of Military Service* (Beverly Hills, CA: SAGE, 1976), 119–23; and Willie M. Turner and Lois A. West, "Violence in Military Families," *Response to Violence in the Family* 4 (May/June 1981), 1.

2. "First National Conference on Violence in Military Families," *Response to Violence in the Family* 4 (March/April 1981), 1.

3. Letter to the authors from David R. Segal, Professor of Sociology and Government and Politics, University of Maryland, 29 May 1984.

4. John H. Farris, "The Impact of Basic Combat Training: The Role of the Drill Sergeant," in Goldman and Segal, *The Social Psychology of Military Service,* 14–15.

5. Morris Janowitz, *The Professional Soldier* (Glencoe, IL.: The Free Press, 1960), 32.

6. Peter H. Neidig and Dale H. Friedman, *Spouse Abuse—A Treatment Program for Couples* (Champaign, IL.: Research Press, 1984), 114–15.

7. M. Duncan Stanton, "The Military Family: Its Future in the All-Volunteer Context," in Goldman and Segal, *The Social Psychology of Military Service,* 135–38.

8. For a discussion of the general strains affecting the military family, see Raymond M. Marsh, "Mobility in the Military: Its Effect upon the Family System," in Hamilton I. McMubbin, Barbara B. Dahl, and Edna J. Hunter, eds., *Families in the Military System* (Beverly Hills, CA: SAGE, 1976), 92–111; and Nancy K. Raiha, "Spouse Abuse in the Military Community: Factors Influencing Incidence and Treatment," in Maria Roy, ed., *The Abusive Partner* (New York: Van Nostrand Reinhold, 1982), 103–25. On wives' alcoholism, see Gerald R. Garrett et. al, "Drinking and the Military Wife: A Study of Married Women in Overseas Base Communities." in Edna J. Hunter and D. Stephen Nice, eds., *Military Families* (New York: Praeger Press, 1978), 222–37. Edna J. Hunter [*Families Under the Flag* (New York: Praeger Press, 1978), 26] observes that the military alcoholism rate for both men and women is three times that of the general population.

9. Edna J. Hunter, *Families Under the Flag,* 9.

10. Stanton, "The Military Family," 158.

11. Our first book, *The Family Secret: Domestic Violence in America* (Boston: Beacon Press, 1983), dealt at length with shelter residences. As at other women's shelters receiving funds from the Texas Department of Human Resources (TDHR), interviews of all incoming clients were required using a standardized form provided by TDHR. We are grateful to Ms. Pat Crawford for making this information available to us.

12. Raiha, "Spouse Abuse in the Military Community," 106–7.

13. Ibid.

14. Joseph A. Califano, Jr., "Doubts About an All-Volunteer Army," in Martin Anderson and Barbara Honegger, eds., *The Military Draft* (Stanford, CA: Stanford University, Hoover Institute Press, 1982), 533.

15. Peter H. Neiding, Dale H. Friedman, and Barbara S. Collins, "Attitudinal Characteristics of Males Who Have Engaged in Spouse Abuse," a paper presented at the Second National Family Violence Research Conference, Durham, NH, August 7–10, 1984.

16. Travis Hirschi and Rodney Stark, "Hellfire and Delinquency," *Social Problems* 17 (Fall 1969), 202–13.

17. Rodney Stark, "Religion and Conformity: Reaffirming a Sociology of Religion," *Sociological Analysis* 45 (Winter 1984), 274–5.

Chapter 5
Religion and Family Violence

1. J. Gordon Melton, "Cult-Related Violence," a paper presented at a conference titled "Other Religions: Other Realities," University of Nebraska, Lincoln, NE, March 1985.

2. Janet Jacobs, "The Economy of Love in Religious Commitment: The Deconversion of Women From NonTraditional Religious Movements," *Journal for the Scientific Study of Religion* 23 (June 1984), 155–71.

3. Karl Marx, *Karl Marx on Religion*. Edited and translated by Saul K. Padover (New York: McGraw-Hill, 1974), xx.

4. 1 Tim. 2:9–12.

5. 1 Cor. 14:34–5.

6. Erling Jorstad, *Evangelicals in the White House: The Cultural Maturation of Born Again Christianity 1960–1981* (New York: The Edwin Mellen Press, 1981), 101.

7. Charles R. Jeffords, "The Impact of Sex-Role and Religious Attitudes Upon Forced Marital Intercourse Norms," *Sex Roles* 11 (September 1984), 543–52.

8. Karen Willoughby, "Common Ground: Speakers Minimize Their Husbands Ideological Differences," *Fort Worth Star-Telegram,* 20 April 1985.

9. Gal. 3:27–8.

10. See Rosemary Radford Ruether and Rosemary Skinner Keller, eds., *Women and Religion in America,* vol 1 of *The Nineteenth Century* (San Francisco: Harper & Row, 1981).

11. Murray A. Straus, Richard J. Gelles, and Suzanne K. Steinmetz, *Behind Closed Doors: Violence in the American Family* (New York: Doubleday, 1980), 138.

12. Church religiosity was measured by giving a respondent a point if he or she was a member of a church, another point if he or she could name its denomination, then points for frequency of church attendance (3 points for every week, 2 points for only now and then, 1 point for very seldom and 0 points for not at all) and making financial contributions to the church (3 points for at least once a week, 2 points for 1 or 2 times a month, 1 point for several times a year, and 0 points for almost never). Physical violence was measured by thirteen questionnaire items that asked if the respondent had ever been pushed, grabbed, or shoved; been struck with hands, feet, or objects; been threatened with weapons; sustained various types of injuries or medical treatment for them; been forced to have sexual intercourse; called the police, and so forth. For specific details on this questionnaire, see Richard N. Breen, *Premarital Violence: A Study of Abuse Within the Dating Relationships of College Students,* unpublished master's thesis, The University of Texas at Arlington, May 1985.

13. Jacobs, "The Economy of Love in Religious Commitment," 164.

14. Ibid.

15. *Family Life: A Resolution* (Nashville TN: The United Methodist Church, Family Life Committee, 1980), 8.

16. Dean M. Kelley, *Why Conservative Churches Are Growing,* rev. ed. (San Francisco: Harper & Row, 1977).

17. See David G. Bromley and Anson Shupe, eds., *New Christian Politics* (Macon, GA: Mercer University Press, 1984); and Robert C. Liebman and Robert Wuthnow, eds., *The New Christian Right* (New York: Aldine, 1983).

Chapter 6
Breaking the Cycle of Family Violence

1. Melissa J. Eddy and Toby Myers, *Helping Men Who Batter: A Profile of Programs in the U.S.* (Austin, TX: Texas Department of Human Resources, 1984).

2. See Richard Gelles, "Abused Wives: Why Do They Stay," *Journal of Marriage and the Family* 38, no. 4 (November 1976), 659–68. Of fifty-four women who never saw such parental violence, about one-half were battered.

3. Mildred Daley Pagelow, *Family-Battering: Victims and Their Experiences* (Beverly Hills, CA: SAGE, 1981), 163–77; and William A. Stacey and Anson Shupe, *The Family Secret: Domestic Violence in America* (Boston: Beacon Press, 1983), 90–94.

4. Richard J. Gelles, "Applying Research on Family Violence to Clinical Practice," *Journal of Marriage and the Family* 44 no. 1 (February 1982), 9–20.

5. Lawrence W. Sherman and Richard A. Berk, "The Specific Deterrent Effects of Arrest for Domestic Assaults," *American Sociological Review* 49 no. 2 (April 1984), 1261–72.

6. The detailed technical results of this follow-up study are published in *An Evaluation of Three Programs for Abusive Men in Texas* (October 1984), available from the Texas Department of Human Resources, Austin, Texas. They are presented in *Research Monograph No. 29* of the Division of Family Life, Center For Social Research, The University of Texas at Arlington.

7. In recent years extensive research has documented the cost-effective advantages of conducting telephone interviews instead of the more traditional face-to-face type. In cases where sensitive topics are being discussed and where rapport between a respondent and interviewer representing a trusted agency has been established, the telephone format may produce more candor. Such rapport was not difficult for our interviewers to establish, considering that before each interview, the interviewer had read over the past client's file and therefore already knew a great deal about the person. On the advantages of telephone interviewing, see James H. Frey, *Survey Research by Telephone* (Beverly Hills, CA: SAGE, 1983); Lawrence A. Jordon, Alfred C. Marcus, and Leo G. Reeder, "Response Styles in Telephone and Household Interviewing: A Field Experiment," *Public Opinion Quarterly* 44 no. 2 (1980) Summet 210–22; and Robert Groves and Robert L. Kahn, *Surveys by Telephone: A National Comparison with Personal Interviews* (New York: Academic Press, 1979).

8. Fewer women were located because in cases of divorce or separation, they frequently returned home to their parents or other relatives, who often lived in other communities if not in other states.

9. Table 6–4 presents evidence on the handful of women who reported that child abuse occurred after men left counseling. Suffice it to say that there does not seem to be any reason to see this problem as something critical for most men after counseling at least in this sample.

10. Letter of Edward W. Gondolf, Indiana University of Pennsylvania, to Deborah Tucker, executive associate, Texas Council of Family Violence, 10 January 1985. Copy provided to us by the author.

11. Sherman and Berk, "The Specific Deterrent Effects of Arrest for Domestic Assaults," 1261–72.

12. Edward Gondolf, *Men Who Batter: Why They Abuse Women and How They Stop Their Abuse* (Indiana, PA: Domestic Violence Study Center, Indiana University of Pennsylvania, 1984).

Chapter 7
Antiviolence Strategies at the Community Level

1. Janet A. Geller and Janice Wasserstrom, "Cojoint Therapy for the Treatment of Domestic Violence," in Albert R. Roberts, ed., *Battered Women and Their Families* (New York: Springer Publishing Company, 1984), 33–48.

2. Interview with Allen Dietz, psychologist, Austin Police Department, summer 1982.

3. *Under the Rule of Thumb: Battered Women and the Administration of Justice: A Report of the United States Commission on Civil Rights* (Washington, DC: U.S. Government Printing Office, 1982), 82.

4. Mike Royko, "Goetz Taught Punks a Valuable Lesson." *Fort Worth Star-Telegram* (17 January 1985), 2.

Index

About the Authors

Anson Shupe received his doctorate from Indiana University in 1975. He is currently Professor of Sociology at the University of Texas at Arlington and Associate Director of the Center for Social Research there. A prolific author, he co-authored (with William A. Stacey) *The Family Secret: Domestic Violence in America* and has written more than a dozen other books dealing with national and international social movements.

William A. Stacey received his doctorate from Florida State University in 1970. He is currently Associate Professor of Sociology at the University of Texas at Arlington and serves as Director of that institution's Center for Social Research. In addition to co-authoring *The Family Secret,* he has written on criminology, race relations, and co-authored (with Anson Shupe) *Born Again Politics and the Moral Majority: What Social Surveys Really Show.*

Lonnie R. Hazlewood received his Master of Science in Health Professions from Southwest Texas State University in 1980. Co-Founder and Director of the Austin Stress Clinic, he is also Coordinator of the Family Violence Diversion Network of the Austin Child and Family Service. His specialties include stress management, anger control, and biofeedback uses in counseling.